C000217398

100 Unhip Albums
THAT WE SHOULD LEARN TO LOVE

IAN KEITH MOSS

EMPIRE
PUBLICATIONS

First published in 2019

EMPIRE PUBLICATIONS
1 Newton Street, Manchester M1 1HW
© Ian Moss 2019

ISBN: 978-1-909360-71-6

Contents

Acknowledgements 5

Foreword by Ged Babey 5

About the Author by Bob Osborne 9

1. Leo Sayer - Silverbird (1973) 11

2. Neil Young & Crazy Horse - Greendale (2003) 12

3. King Crimson - THRAK (1995) 14

4. Tangerine Dream - Electronic Meditation (1970) 15

5. Scissor Sisters - Night Work (2010) 17

6. Larry Young - Lawrence Of Newark (1973) 18

7. Status Quo - Blue For You (1976) 20

8. David Essex - David Essex (1974) 21

9. Tricky - Pre-Millennium Tension (1996) 23

10. Edgar Broughton Band - Edgar Broughton Band (1971) . 24

11. Major Lance
    - His Greatest Hits Live At The Torch (1973) 26

12. Wilco - Summerteeth (1999) 28

13. Pulp - We Love Life (2001) 30

14. David Bowie - Let's Dance (1983) 32

15. Basement Jaxx - Rooty (2001) 34

16. Love - Four Sail (1969) 35

17. Pink Grease - This Is For Real (2004) 37

18. Barry White - Stone Gon' (1973) 38

19. Bob Dylan - Self Portrait (1970) 40

20. Lindisfarne - Nicely Out Of Tune (1970) 42

21. The Groundhogs - Split (1971) 44

22. Lou Reed & Metallica - Lulu (2011) 46

23. Van Der Graaf Generator - Godbluff (1975) 48

24. Slade - Alive! (1972) 50

25. Bryan Ferry- These Foolish Things (1973) 52

26. Diana Ross - Diana (1980) 54

27. Saturday Night Fever Soundtrack (1977) 56

28. The Mekons - The Curse Of The Mekons (1991) 58

29. The Style Council
  - Introducing The Style Council (1983) 60
30. Cat Stevens - Mona Bone Jakon (1970) 62
31. Konono N°1 - Congotronics (2004) 64
32. Argent - Encore (Live in Concert) (1974) 65
33. Electric Light Orchestra - Eldorado (1974) 67
34. The Vibrators - Pure Mania (1977) 69
35. Wings - Wildlife (1971)..71
36. MC 900 ft. Jesus with DJ Zero
  - Hell With The Lid Off (1990) 73
37. The Stylistics - The Stylistics (1971).........................74
38. 10cc - Sheet Music (1974)......................................76
39. Win - ...Uh! Tears Baby (1987) 78
40. Cockney Rebel - The Psychomodo (1974)..................79
41. Poet And The Roots
  - Dread Beat an' Blood (1978)..................................81
42. ABBA - Voulez-Vous (1979)...................................82
43. The Carpenters - A Song For You (1972)....................84
44. Pearls Before Swine
  - One Nation Underground (1967) 85
45. Jerry Lee Lewis
  - Live At The Star Club, Hamburg (1964) 87
46. Adam And The Ants
  - Kings Of The Wild Frontier (1980) 89
47. Jellyfish - Bellybutton (1990) 91
48. Screaming Blue Messiahs - Good And Gone (1984) 92
49. Al Green - The Belle Album (1977)...........................94
50. The Shadows - The Shadows (1961)..........................95
51. World Of Twist - Quality Street (1991)......................96
52. Gene Vincent And His Blue Caps
  - Gene Vincent And His Blue Caps (1957) 98
53. The Cannonball Adderley Quintet
  - Accent On Africa (1968) 100
54. Bob Marley and The Wailers - Natty Dread (1974).......101
55. Elvis Presley - Elvis Is Back! (1960).........................103
56. The Who - Tommy (1969)......................................105

57. Montrose - Montrose (1973) 107
58. The Kinks - Muswell Hillbillies (1971).......................109
59. Frankie Goes To Hollywood
  - Welcome To The Pleasuredome (1984)..........................111
60. Sinéad O'Connor
  - I Do Not Want What I Haven't Got (1990).................113
61. Elvis Costello and The Attractions
  - Blood and Chocolate (1986).....................................114
62. Elton John - Goodbye Yellow Brick Road (1973) 116
63. Gilbert O'Sullivan - Himself (1971)...........................117
64. The Saints - Prehistoric Sounds (1978).......................119
65. Nic Jones - Penguin Eggs (1980)...............................121
66. Them - The Angry Young Them (1965).......................122
67. Dory Previn - Mythical Kings and Iguanas (1971)........123
68. The Fatima Mansions - Viva Dead Ponies (1991) 125
69. Stackridge - Stackridge (1971) 126
70. Kevin Ayers - The Unfairground (2007) 127
71. Cornershop - Handcream For A Generation (2002) 129
72. Lynyrd Skynyrd - One More from the Road (1976).......130
73. Billy Fury - The Sound of Fury (1960)......................132
74. The Monkees - The Monkees (1966) 133
75. T. Rex - Futuristic Dragon (1976) 135
76. Imagination - Body Talk (1981) 136
77. The Auteurs - After Murder Park (1996)....................138
78. Mungo Jerry - Electronically Tested (1971) 139
79. Laura Nyro
  - Eli and the Thirteenth Confession (1968) 141
80. Howard Tate - Get it While You Can (1966)...............143
81. ELP - - Trilogy (1972)...145
82. Kevin Rowland - My Beauty (1999) 147
83. Robert Calvert - Lucky Leif and the Longships (1975)...149
84. Television Personalities - My Dark Places (2006) 151
85. The Residents - Eskimo (1979)................................153
86. Neil Diamond - Hot August Night (1972)..................154
87. The Go-Betweens - Oceans Apart (2005) 156
88. Bim Sherman - Miracle (1996)................................158

89. Bill Withers - Still Bill (1972)................................159

90. Rahsaan Roland Kirk
   - The Case of the 3 Sided Dream in Audio Color (1975)...160

91. Free - The Free Story (1973)....................................162

92. Cecil Taylor - Unit Structures (1966)..........................164

93. Mott the Hoople - Mott the Hoople (1969).................165

94. Kevin Coyne - Marjory Razorblade (1973).................167

95. Vangelis - See You Later (1980)................................168

96. The Prick Jaggers - The Golden Ass (2006).................170

96. Doll by Doll - Gypsy Blood (1979)...........................172

98. The Beatles
   - Sgt. Pepper's Lonely Hearts Club Band (1967)............174

99. Lord Sutch - And Heavy Friends (1970)....................176

100. Root Boy Slim and the Sex Change Band
   - Zoom (1979)..178

101. Metal Urbain
   - Les Hommes Mort Sont Dangereux (1980).................180

102. Stealers Wheel - Stealers Wheel (1972)....................181

103. Subway Sect - Sansend (2002)...............................183

104. Bread - Bread (1969)...185

105. Queen - Sheer Heart Attack (1972).........................186

106. Glen Campbell
   - Reunion: The Songs of Jimmy Webb (1972).................188

107. PJ Proby - Heroes (1998).....................................189

108. The Barmy Army - The English Disease (1989)..........192

109. Family - Fearless (1971).....................................193

110. Rod Stewart - A Night on the Town (1976)..............195

Acknowledgements

Thanks to Mick Middles for the encouragement to undertake this writing and to Ciaran Humphries for support, suggestions and practical assistance without whom this work would have remained no more than an idle thought

Foreword

"There is one thing you should know:
what is hip today might become passé"

What is Hip?
Tower of Power 1973

"In '87, Huey (Lewis & the News) released this ... Fore!, their most accomplished album. I think their undisputed masterpiece is 'Hip to Be Square,' a song so catchy, most people probably don't listen to the lyrics. But they should, because it's not just about the pleasures of conformity, and the importance of trends, it's also a personal statement about the band itself."

Patrick Bateman,
"American Psycho" by Brett Easton Ellis

THIS IS NOT A BOOK about so-called 'guilty pleasures'. There is absolutely no shame involved at all – just pure, unadulterated, unfettered pleasure. Nor is this a consumer guide. There are no details of reissue dates, catalogue numbers and the best place to buy. Just find your nearest second-hand music shop – or try charity shops and boot-sales. This is a book for music lovers and fanatics rather than music snobs; people with huge record collections, but those who don't strategically place the 'coolest' most fashionable records at the front, in case someone should pop round.

This book contains 100★ mini-essays about albums which the taste-makers and purveyors of received wisdom probably wouldn't want you to hear. The albums are not part of The Canon (the Beatles *Revolver*, the Beach Boys *Smile*, Van Morrison *Astral Weeks*… you know, The Top 100 Greatest Albums). These albums are over-looked, because for some reason they didn't sell a lot or the critics gave them short shrift. They were not 'cool' or the artist lacked a reputation or was considered past their prime. Then there are the records that were lauded when they first came out but have since been re-assessed as 'uncool'. That doesn't mean they are not brilliant, inspirational and total classic, it's just that no-one has pointed it out before.

To decide what is 'unhip', we have to first establish what exactly 'hip' means. It comes from 'hep' or hep-cat, jazz lingo from the 1930's, the kind of 'solid gone daddio' slang used by beatniks and Baloo from Disney's cartoon of *Jungle Book*. One derivation comes from fashionable opium-users who would stretch out whilst indulging, laying 'on the hip'.

This would explain why Modern Jazz and Lou Reed and the Velvet Underground are considered perennially hip. Drug use and sunglasses after dark always seem to be an indicator of hipness. The opposite to hip is of course square, which Huey Lewis insisted was momentarily, in his mind, hip. An assertion only a psychopath would take seriously. Things go in and out of fashion. Styles are revived and recycled. 'What is considered hip is continuously changing' it says in Wikipedia.

Ian Moss has never given a monkey's about what was fashionable – if he likes it, he likes it –and wants to know more about it; the song, the album, the artist. An avid reader of the music press, he has an encyclopedic knowledge and eclectic taste. You will find every genre covered here.

Daily postings on social media about whatever he was listening to that day resulted in this book. Nearly every album has a memory or anecdote attached, putting it in context and pinpointing why the album is a worthwhile listen.

Ian is a man of wisdom and taste; a champion of the underdog, a believer in 'no-rules' only the freedom to express yourself. There is no ulterior motive to this book, no tie-in with a re-issue record label. No scores to settle. Only passion, with a disregard for fashion.

He is opinionated, but usually right, and funny, knowledgeable and entertaining with it. *100 Unhip Albums* is a great read and there's plenty of music to seek out and listen to afterwards.

The irony is that Ian rails against 'received wisdom' and the opinion of taste-makers, yet here he is putting his wisdom in this book-shaped receptacle and hoping that you find his opinion of value and his taste agreeable.

So, tuck in, and drink the long draught (man) to the Unhip Priest.

Ged Babey, April 2019

(louderthanwar.com/author/ged-babey/)

About the Author

by Bob Osborne

IN A CITY THAT has had more than its fair share of musical heroes, who have achieved both national and international recognition, Ian Moss remains a less well-known but steadfast figure in the Manchester musical underground. In equal parts an innovator and an agitator, a protagonist and a game changer, he has steadfastly followed a unique and paradigm shifting path. As one of the handful of people who were actually at the first Sex Pistols gig at the Lesser Free Trade Hall in Manchester in 1976, and the co-creator of the legendary band Hamsters, that John Peel described as being too "dark and dangerous" to appear on his show, Ian has often found himself at the cusp of key events in the evolution of music in the city.

Visit Ian at home, and you will find a man immersed in music. Whether it be the copious books that line his shelves, or the seemingly endless cabinets filled to the brim with Vinyl and CDs, where a Sun Ra box set sits easily alongside a collection of rare Stooges recordings, his home is a living museum to the music of the last 75 years. Rock, punk, jazz, blues, soul (especially Northern), and experimental music are all there. Stockhausen can be heard alongside David Essex, Kevin Ayers follows Van Der Graaf Generator, there are no barriers, no restrictions, and few favourites.

Ian has absorbed and translated the musical culture of the city of Manchester and its surrounding settlements with vigour since the 1970s. Whether it be debating the merits of the Flamin' Groovies with Mark E Smith, touring with The Mekons and acting as a body double for Jon Langford, appearing on television and radio to discuss the post-punk explosion, or creating the opportunity for some of the most exciting, albeit unknown to the wider public, bands the city has enjoyed, Moss has been there. He has consistently championed the grass roots of music. As the vocalist and lyricist of bands like Stepbrothers, Sicknurse, Kill Pretty, and currently, Four Candles, Ian has realised his own musical vision. But he has also created opportunities and spaces for other bands and artists as the founder and co-owner of the German Shepherd Record label which for the last five years has released unique and ground-breaking music to great critical acclaim. His Manchester Meltdown events over the last two years have brought together some of the best music in the city with no barriers associated with age, hipness, or the perceived notion of what is 'happening'.

Sit in a pub with Ian and discuss music and you will find yourself agreeing and disagreeing with his opinions in equal measure, but you will be educated and entertained. This book reflects a man who loves music and wants to share it. It also reflects someone who has spent his life championing the music that most people don't get to hear. In a world where access to music is easier than it has ever been, and where vast choices are available, Moss is uniquely positioned as a commentator on those things you might have missed.

To paraphrase one of Ian's greatest lyrics "everything's permitted at any given time", this book celebrates musical diversity and encourages wider listening.

1. Leo Sayer
Silverbird (1973)

Think Leo Sayer and picture the curly-mopped, inanely grinning MoR balladeer and faux disco poppet dancing on the ceiling in an inverted world of tame family-orientated TV shows of the late 70's.

It's difficult to remember that when he emerged with this debut album, *Silverbird* in 1973 he was viewed very differently. Sayer and his song-writing partner David Courtney had gained attention and lavish praise by writing the bulk of Roger Daltrey's first solo record that had been a major commercial and critical success.

The beautiful and poignant, *"Why Is Everybody Going Home"* had been released as a single and flopped, its fragile mournfulness failing to gain radio airplay but Sayer's tour as main support to Roxy Music was begun and *"The Show Must Go On"* issued as a single simultaneously to the album release. The single was strikingly original, Sayer in full Pierrot outfit and makeup cut a striking and somewhat sinister figure, the nation was captivated and it propelled both single and album to number two in their respective charts.

The album seemed to herald a major talent, albeit shakily produced by Courtney and sixties icon Adam Faith who was holding the management reins. The songs were excellent and varied and Sayer's voice rich, expressive and capable of going from a throaty rasp to a tender croon as recurring themes of loneliness and despair were played out. The opening track, *"Innocent Bystander"* sets the tone well and paints a picture of a man waiting for something good to happen and despairing that it never will to the point he is *"Going Out Of His Head"*. The next track, *"Goodnight Old Friend"* is another lament with shifts in tempo hinting at the emotional imbalance of the protagonist. *"Drop back"* is the first of the rockers that are scattered across the platter and though they seem to lack some of the authentic grit of road-hardened bands who had paid their dues (the same lack of authenticity could be levelled at the likes of David Bowie where this perceived weakness became in fact a strength by emphasising an otherworldly quality), closing side one *"The Show Must Go On"* which put paranoia into the charts and *"The Dancer"* where Sayer sings in falsetto the tragic tale of the fall of a high wire dancer over a dramatic orchestrated piece, it is a stunning, devastating and beautiful piece of music.

Side two in truth doesn't live up to the excellence of side one. Not that it goes dramatically wrong at all, *"Don't Say It's Over"* and the aforementioned *"Why Is Everybody Going Home"* are both sad and delicate songs handled with sensitivity and finesse whilst *"Tomorrow"* and *"Oh Wot A Life"* are brisk and jaunty workouts that give the album, as a whole, balance.

Sayer's world changed with this success and his writing never contained the sadness and sensitivity that it did on this quite exquisite album.

2. Neil Young & Crazy Horse
Greendale (2003)

It's not so often one gets the chance to see Neil Young and Crazy Horse perform live and to see them in the relatively intimate setting of Manchester's two-thousand capacity Apollo Theatre was indeed a rare and eagerly anticipated treat. And so we gathered and witnessed a show that deeply divided the audience as the forthcoming Greendale album was performed in its entirety, I personally was utterly captivated.

Neil was clearly having a ball and was most certainly not going through the motions as he narrated the confusing tale between songs where he frequently unleashed his oddly beautiful clunking guitar riffs atop Crazy Horses behind the beat soulful stumble. There was occasional audible dissatisfaction from displeased audience members. Greendale finished and there was an interval where the level of anger at the performance was aired in many conversations. I kind of hoped the second half of the show would mirror what had happened on the *"Tonight's the Night"* tour thirty years before when disgruntled audiences were promised by Young, "…Something you've heard before…" and played the exact same set in repeat, again rather than the hits they wanted to hear!

On this occasion Neil gave the audience what they actually wanted and although hearing his classic songs played was fine, though it felt like an anti-climax to my ears after the freshness of the opening set.

The album, *Greendale* followed. It is a cycle of songs based around an extended family in the imaginary Californian town of Greendale. A convoluted tale taking on love, murder, ecological issues and the weight of big business and big money bearing down on "little people". As a story it fails dismally as the narrative meanders and a plot is either absent or lost in the labyrinth of dead ends. But none of that truly matters because it lends Neil a theme to write around. He was most certainly engaged by the concept and there were no moments on the record where he coasted as he had been prone to for a decade or more. Here he is saying what he wishes to say, he's not an elegant florid writer but the awkward fit of his words and his conversational delivery are gripping, add the rugged sound that he and Crazy Horse conjure up that is full of emotion and nobility means this is a remarkable life-affirming record.

This works best as an album, all seventy-plus minutes of it, rather than a series of tracks which is perhaps why the material here doesn't get aired in live performances these days or make radio playlists but attention should be drawn to *"Bandit"*, one of this consummate artist's true classics.

3. King Crimson
THRAK (1995)

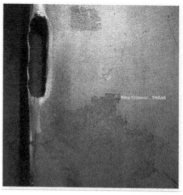

King Crimson are not unhip. Far from it in fact! They are a name a hipster can drop casually into conversation to confer instant cool. For Crimson without being obscure are something of the connoisseur's choice. Despite this fact, it does tend to be only two periods of the band's history that are revered. Either the late sixties/early seventies majestic progressive era of *In The Court Of The Crimson King* through to *Larks Tongues In Aspic* or the later seventies early eighties brittle funky art rock of albums like *Red* and *Discipline*. What came later is left in a dusty cupboard and is largely unloved, deemed as difficult and ugly, it has no place among the vinyl re-pressings that signify studied 'edgy good taste'.

Exhibit A is this album, stylised as THRAK in bold capitals, that came after a decade-long silence, with the exception of a mini-album released in 1994, a companion and preamble to *THRAK*. All of the tracks on *Vrooom* (with the exception of *"Cage"* and *"When I Say Stop, Continue"*) reappeared on *THRAK* as different recordings.

Here Fripp assembled a six-piece team of players including long term Crimson personnel in drummer Bill Bruford, bassist Tony Levin and guitarist/vocalist Adrian Belew. Added to them are bassist Trey Gunn and percussionist Pat Mastelotto, meaning each instrument is doubled up on, split them and you have a double trio!

The opening track *"VROOOM"* displays the possibilities of this format to the full, starting as a vicious head-on aural assault and midway through, the two trios separate. Each plays through a different channel to devastating mind-spinning effect. The music on the instrumental sections is often dense but this is not the thrash of joyous noise for noise's sake, listen and it is apparent that each instrument has its place in the mix as they twist and twine around each other.

This is the sound of a band a quarter of a century into its existence yet still moving forward, still progressing. It is thrilling, daredevil stuff; a mixture of the cerebral and physical that is pulled off with aplomb, the instrumental tracks interspersed with vocals only songs to give breathing space and balance to the album as a whole. *"Dinosaur"* and *"Sex Sleep Eat Drink Dream"* certainly work as stand alone tracks.

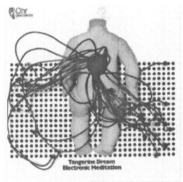

4. Tangerine Dream
Electronic Meditation
(1970)

This was the debut album of Tangerine Dream with a line-up of Edgar Froese on guitar and various effects, Klaus Shultze on drums, Conrad Schnitzler playing cello and violin with guest musicians playing organ and flute (both featuring prominently). This line-up would only last until the end of the recording process before splintering.

This comes as little surprise when listening to this record, the level of intense playing could surely not be contained within a single unit for long. Anyone coming to this album from hearing the records made in their successful mid-seventies Virgin Records period is in for a huge shock because the tranquil floating new-ageish beauty of albums like *Phaedra* and *Rubycon* is completely absent on this early work.

Here they revel in noise and spontaneity as they strive for

free expression. If you were to imagine the MC5's mighty *"Kick Out The Jams"* being recorded not by young Americans from industrial Detroit in thrall to the Music of Sun Ra and Ornette Colman but by disaffected German youths in the divided city of Berlin influenced in equal parts by Karlheinz Stockhausen and Jimi Hendrix, you're getting close to the sound of *"Electronic Meditation"*. In the U.K. Pink Floyd were inching toward this direction but sounded cautious, unsure of themselves and timid. Tangerine Dream were going straight for the jugular, determined to make every note count.

The album opens with cello giving way to free-form guitar before Shultze introduces a huge tribal beat to proceedings; flute and organ further enhance the sound that builds before all it can do is collapse. The thirteen minute epic *"Journey Through A Burning Brain"* follows, it is perhaps the most comfortable track here for fans of orthodox rock in that guitars scream and drums thunder furiously, it's a thrilling acid tinged ride. *"Cold Smoke"* follows, it's another epic trip of a track where jams build and fade away to be replaced by new ones rising from the feeding-back guitars. Next comes the organ-led *"Ashes to Ashes"* which reaches apocalyptic proportions before some backtracked vocals launch us into the final track *"Resurrection"* which burns like a Roman candle.

I once guested on a radio programme where I chose the music, most of which delighted the presenter until I passed him this album and asked him to play *"Ashes to Ashes"*. He was horrified even asking, "...Isn't there something we can play instead?" I was insistent and as the track played he expressed surprise remarking, "It's good this! Not what I was expecting". Tangerine Dream have not been on any hipster radar for many a decade, but I am absolutely sure they will be rediscovered and Bohemian types will once more proudly drop their name.

5. Scissor Sisters
Night Work
(2010)

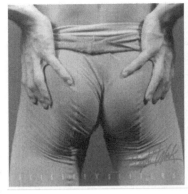

The cover art alone made the statement that this is a queer album, not an all-inclusive album with a few sanitised gay themes but an explicitly gay piece of work, which might well leave a large chunk of the band's established audience feeling they were on the outside looking in.

One attempt to record the album was scrapped as unsatisfactory and a number of songs previewed live for possible inclusion wouldn't make the cut. Jake Shears followed the David Bowie/Iggy Pop route and decamped to Berlin for a two-month sabbatical and one can detect that city's atmosphere seeping into the creative process. Stuart Price, responsible for the sound on Madonna's magnificent 2005 album *"Confessions On A Dance Floor"*, was brought in to produce and this harder-edged album was the result.

From the opening title track a template is set, everything is fuller sounding and more beat driven. This doesn't let-up, the whole album is full of tracks that can be danced to, mirroring the clubbing experience. Where on previous records the influence of Elton John and ABBA had lent a melodic mass appeal, here they are almost non-existent and what is evoked is a pre-AIDS Crisis clubland of hedonistic excess. That excess is soured by loneliness and a feeling that there must be more than endlessly seeking out anonymous fleeting sexual liaisons.

Lyrically the record is highly sexualised and littered with a phalanx of metaphors for the sex act but none of this is used for cheap or smutty titillation but rather as an honest representation of gay night-life and the urge for connection and intimacy. This is encapsulated on *"Skin Tight"* which concerns itself with condom use and *"Sex And Violence"* about the S&M scene. The album concludes with a darker cousin of Michael Jackson's *"Thriller"* that features Ian McKellen voicing a celebration of the 'bacchanal'.

The record was as emphatic a success artistically as could have been hoped but relatively speaking a failure commercially in comparison to the success enjoyed by their first two albums, but this was the album where we were allowed into the heart of the Scissor Sisters. This was the album where their soul was bared, it was the album the band needed to make to be true to themselves. A brave undertaking and a complete triumph.

6. Larry Young
Lawrence Of Newark (1973)

Any hipster worth their salt will profess to dig Jazz. From the bebop wordplay of Ginsberg and Burroughs through to the influence on the French new wave film auteurs such as Godard, the mod movement and the undeniable debt much of hip-hop owes to it, Jazz has always been a badge to be worn that confers cool.

That the genre draws this attention is a positive thing without doubt, but the negative is all too often the appreciation of the form by the white bourgeois "cool" is almost entirely superficial so they may allow albums by Miles Davis, John Coltrane, Billie Holiday etc, into their boho living quarters and enjoy the ambiance of some smooth cocktail-type Jazz as background noise in the coffee shop or micro-pub they're frequenting, but care little for anything beyond that. What they are missing is a treasure chest of creativity and expressiveness and of which this album by Larry Young is a fine example.

Young was an organist and occasional pianist who, in the late fifties and early sixties, recorded a series of albums featuring himself at the Hammond performing Soul-Jazz grooves, not dissimilar to Jimmy Smith, signing to Blue Note Records in 1964. Clearly influenced by the direction John Coltrane had pursued, Young's music became much more adventurous and free-form. He recorded a bunch of albums of high quality including the classic *Unity.*

Toward the end of the sixties he joined drummer Tony Williams and guitarist John McLaughlin in Jazz fusion pioneering band Lifetime, then moved onto Miles's band to help record *Bitches Brew* and cut a jam with Jimi Hendrix. In 1973 he signed to Perception Records to make his first album in five years as a band leader. He recruited mostly young players from New York on the fringes of the Funk Jazz scene including the inimitable guitar great James 'Blood' Ulmer, trumpeter Charles McGee, a whole assembly of drummer/percussionists and Pharoah Saunders on tenor sax.

The record they made was extraordinary, showcasing the organ in a way it had not been used before and creating a darkly psychedelic masterpiece that coils and shape-shifts as it switches tempos and mood, moving from Eastern drones to intense rhythmic attack. The five tracks on the album never stay in one place, never allow you to get to comfortable, the music keeps moving. The finest example being on the second track of the record *"Khalid Of Space Part Two"*, where the musical landscape is very strange indeed; congos, bells and all manner of percussion drift in and out without derailing the momentum of the piece as both Young's keyboard and Blood Ulmer's guitar are used to accentuate the rhythm. It is a titanic piece that sets the mind spinning and blood racing suggesting endless possibilities. It is the outstanding track of a truly outstanding album that was for many years almost forgotten, as the label closed down within weeks of its release. It is a record that deserves to be cherished.

7. Status Quo
Blue For You (1976)

When arch-hipster Damon Albarn, at the height of the stupid media war of the horrid Brit-pop years, christened his rivals "Quoasis" it was clearly not meant as a compliment. It was used to denigrate and suggest the mono-browed brothers were unimaginative and a bit naff! He was spot-on in that assessment of course, but to use Status Quo to illustrate his point simply showed him as an ignorant snob.

Blue for You was the last of Quo's classic period albums; all self-produced and self-written. Later in the year they would release the defining keyboard-led *"Rockin' All Over The World"* and become mainstream pop stars but that's getting ahead of ourselves. Here the four-piece of Rossi, Parfitt, Coghlan and Lancaster do what they had been doing since 1971's *"Piledriver"*, they play long intros that bear little relationship to the main song that suddenly end to reveal a pulverising riff. They find time to include a track so untypical (in this case, *"Ease your Mind"*) you'd be forgiven for thinking they'd lost the plot and finish the album with the longest song on the album, *"Mystery Song"*.

I must give mention to opening track *"Is There A Better Way"* with a sound that in twelve months' time would be replicated by younger, shorter-haired bands at the Roxy club and elsewhere. Also *"Rain"*, the main single from this album that contained none of the Quo anthems, it's a Rick Parfitt written and sung track that is beautifully simple in its relentless chugging guitar riffing but I find incredibly uplifting and in its ability to hit the spot on each listen, quite an emotional experience. There we have it, a fine album from a fine band. Even the hippest of hipsters shouldn't deny themselves the pleasure.

8. David Essex
David Essex (1974)

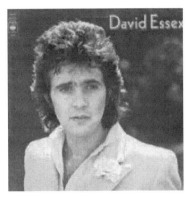

With a succession of flop singles to his name, David Essex took to the boards in thespian mode after landing the lead role in the rock opera *"Godspell"* where he made a name for himself. That led to him starring as Jim McLean in *"That'll Be The Day"*, a film that shows the rise to stardom of an aspiring rocker.

In real life Essex was ready too for another tilt at the record business. With the momentum behind him it was no surprise that this time around the gods smiled on him and he became a huge star. What was surprising though was his sound. I remember reading a review of his comeback single *"Rock On"* where the record was given high praise and a comparison with Captain Beefheart was made. I was fascinated immediately, although Essex was clearly being aimed at a market who lapped up Donny Osmond and David Cassidy, the thought of either of them being compared to the doyenne of the radical alternative seemed absurd.

"Rock on" was of course a superb record announcing Essex in the same way that *"Virginia Plain"* had announced Roxy Music, that is to say audaciously! Sounding like nothing else at all, stripped back, cool and knowing it was post-rock & roll in the midst of a rock & roll revival and propelled Essex immediately into the big time. His follow-up single *"Lamplight"* consolidated as did the debut album which was followed by another film, *"Stardust"*, which was essentially a continuation of *"That'll Be The Day"* where success leads to a hardening of the soul and madness and paranoia ensue. Not exactly teen fodder! But Essex had already been assigned status of manufactured teen idol by the critics. He was never going to appeal to the hirsute denim bedecked rockers

of the day and the cool kids who were glamming up with David Bowie as style icon deemed Essex most unhip.

Like Scott Walker before him, David Essex was trapped in a role that didn't suit him or acknowledge his true merit. In 1974 this self-titled second album followed in the wake of *"Stardust*. It is a sensational album full of dash and daring; the opening track *"Gonna Make You A Star"* became an absolute mega hit as Essex cheekily lampooned the music industry and his position in it, "Is he more than a pretty face?" was the inquiry and "I don't think so" the answer. The sound of the record was phenomenal it was true artistry on the part of producer Jeff Wayne as he channelled elements of Lee Perry's Dub excursions from the Black Ark, Norman Whitfield's psychedelic soul and Conny Plank's thrilling modernity into next track *"Window"* which was inventing a whole new musical language if anyone had cared to listen. *"There's Something About You Baby"* and *"Good Old Rock & Roll"* would have been sure-fire hits if released as singles and that was just side one. *"America"*, a skittish dubby excursion, opens side two and was released as a very strange single that flopped after receiving little airplay.

The album closes with yet another single release, a different take on the movie soundtrack title song *"Stardust"*, quite simply alongside the likes of "Theme From Shaft", *"Heroes"*, *"God Save The Queen"* and *"I Feel Love"* one of the greatest singles in an era of great singles. Underpinned by an amplified human heart beat, Essex wails his existential angst while Chris Spedding wrenches further emotion from the neck of his guitar, there follows a brief cheery refrain of *"Gonna Make You A Star"* and so ends one of the sadly underrated, never hip but ought to be, records of the seventies.

9. Tricky
Pre-Millennium Tension
(1996)

In 1995 Tricky released his debut album, *Maxinquay,* to incredible reviews and sales to match the high praise. He found though that alongside Massive Attack and Portishead, he was being unwillingly categorised as a "Trip Hop" act, expected to provide mellow chill-out music for a generation of ravers seeking a smooth comedown, or worse still, unobtrusive dinner party music for denizens of New Labour's "Cool Britannia" anxious to impress. His music was being reduced to a lifestyle accessory; it was becoming trivialised and he wasn't going to stand for that.

This album simultaneously attempts to reconnect Tricky to his Hip Hop roots whilst also being a very Punk Rock record. Its aim was to free Tricky as an artist so he couldn't be labelled and commodified.

Recorded in Jamaica and New York, Northern Irish guitarist Pat McManus from metal band Mamas Boys featured heavily, the sound he produces is unsettling, contaminating as it fills any empty spaces. As on the first album Martina Topley Bird shares the vocals, acting as a conduit for Tricky's femininity.

This was a heavier more paranoid and claustrophobic record than its predecessor and a closer antecedent would be fellow Bristolians' The Pop Group, rather than Massive Attack, but though the sound changed, the quality certainly didn't drop. This was experimental and serious with barely a chink of light filtered through the darkness and paranoia of tracks such as *"Makes Me Wanna Die"* and the bleak *"Piano"*. Two Hip Hop staples are tackled; Chill Rob G's *"Bad Dreams"* and Eric B and Rakim's *"Lyrics of Fury",* both vocalised by Martina and both seamlessly matching the mood of the album.

This was most certainly not chill out music or dinner party fare, it was an audacious glimpse into a brilliant fractured mind akin to Joseph Conrad's *Heart Of Darkness* anti-hero Colonel Kurtz, it seemed to scream, "Trivialise this! I dare you!" The majority of critics wrote negative reviews and pushed this nasty object aside but they were wrong, this remains a thrilling uncompromising album that sounds just as contemporary now as it did on its release.

10. Edgar Broughton Band

Edgar Broughton Band

(1971)

Before even extracting the vinyl from the record cover, one was almost certainly excited by the sleeve art which repelled many casual browsers with its abattoir scene of a naked human hanging from a meat hook amid rows of slaughtered animals.

It was confrontational in a period when the pretence of the hippy dream of love and peace was the accepted norm. The Broughtons were having none of that, they were questioning political radicals from the tiny freak-scene containing Hawkwind, The Pink Fairies, The Deviants and few others playing free gigs for "the people" often and inspiring love among a small but devoted following (myself included) who found in them honesty and a grip on reality absent elsewhere.

In the hypocritical money-orientated hippie scene, in which the masses were marginalised, patronised and looked down upon for a supposed crudity, the Broughtons offered an alternative. If that preamble makes them sound worthy but perhaps a little dull, forget it! The Edgar Broughton Band were never vanilla, they played hard and soft, loud and quiet, fast and slow and were never pompous.

They were pre-Punk Punks but not Punks like Slaughter and the Dogs or The Lurkers they were musically and spiritually more akin to P.I.L or The Fall.

This was their third LP release in less than two years and their most ambitious and musically varied, ranging from the exquisite orchestral opener *"Evening Over Rooftops"* with an arrangement by David Bedford moonlighting from Kevin Ayers' "The Whole World" to the brutal stomp of *"Don't Even Know What Day It Is"* via the surreal *"Mad Hatter"* and whimsical sing-along *"Poppy"* this was a superlative album containing more wit, wisdom and integrity than truck loads of Pink Floyd or Led Zeppelin records and yet somehow the Broughtons were always treated as inferior, and regarded as little more than a joke.

Perhaps only the endorsement granted by commercial success could have altered that perception and either side of the album release, stand-alone singles might have gate-crashed the charts but twists of fate. Preceding the album was the Captain Beefheart / Shadows hybrid "*Apache Dropout*" which hit number 33 in the charts before losing momentum due to a postal strike which prevented chart returns the next week. The week after the album's release came *"Hotel Room / Call Me A Liar"*; one side stately, the reverse absolutely incendiary which was bizarrely made Tony Blackburn's Record of the Week despite the DJ's unambiguous statement that he "hated all the band stood for". The Edgar Broughton Band were not hip then and have never been posthumously conferred a hip blessing but they were magnificent and that has got to be more important!

Note: *As a fifteen-year-old being sent out to make my way in the world by way of a series of job interviews, I insisted on wearing an Edgar Broughton Band pin badge - it seemed only fair that I send a signal to any prospective employer who recognised that I was part of a mindset that wouldn't simply do as they were told but would question everything. The Edgar Broughton Band conferred on me a rebel spirit and attitude. Misfits they may well have been but this fellow misfit felt the world was a little better for having them around.*

11. Major Lance

His Greatest Hits Live At The Torch (1973)

The Northern Soul scene was the great underground movement of the Seventies. By its very nature it was absolutely anti-authoritarian. To be out getting your kicks in the dead of night, alcohol free but fuelled by pickings of easily burgled chemists, when decent folk were attempting to sleep off a Watney's bitter induced hangover, was hard to understand for straight society. They didn't like what they didn't understand and there was a huge schism between those of "The Faith" who celebrated the forgotten sounds of Black America and those who thought discotheques were for drinking, brawling and ultimately copping off.

That's not to say the Northern Soul scene was a faultless utopia for, despite the love of the music which bonded people from far and wide, there was elitism, intimidation and plenty of unscrupulous characters attracted by the possibility of making big money either from bootlegging records with high price tags or in cutting amphetamine either with harmless talcum powder or the potentially lethal strychnine.

Northern Soul was never album-based, the seven-inch single reigned supreme; the more obscure the better and original pressings were obligatory to have in your collection if you wanted to be taken seriously. It was also records rather than artists that were important, singers who had recorded for a decade or more might have one track deemed worthy of spinning. Who cared about whatever else they'd done? An exception was Major Lance from Chicago and O'Keh records. A contemporary and friend of Curtis Mayfield, the Major had released a string of floor filling "Northern" classics.

Between the closure of the birthplace of the movement, *The Twisted Wheel* club in Manchester, and the opening of the *Casino* club in Wigan which came to be the undisputed Mecca of Soul, the scene had decamped to Tunstall, a satellite of Stoke-on-Trent, at the *Golden Torch*. Among narrow terraced streets the pilgrimage took place each weekend, packing the place and lining the walls with sweat and no night was busier than when Major Lance appeared and was recorded for this album, which while not great in the sense that it improves or even matches his hits, but it provides the most accurate and compelling document of the fervour this music inspired. The roar as the Major takes the stage is only matched by a jet plane taking off and the hand clapping in unison right the way through the performance recalls the response to a Baptist church sermon at its most fiery and gospel infused. The atmosphere was clearly electric and somehow that is captured in the grooves of this record, *"The Beat"*, *"Investigate"* and *"Ain't No Soul"*, all heart-stoppingly brilliant singles, are all carried along by the crowd in almost holy communion with the great legend who was something of a prophet without honour in his homeland.

Northern Soul has fluctuated as a fashion over the decades and even within those who love the genre this album is hardly deemed indispensable but its genius is in capturing a heady night in a heady era in all its blazing glory.

12. Wilco

Summerteeth (1999)

Despite two decades of wilful experimentation and a clear disregard for furthering a career at the expense of their integrity, Wilco seem to be shunted into the corner labelled 'predictable and safe' by influential taste-makers. That attitude towards the band (Jeff Tweedy and others essentially) does them and their music a huge disservice and should be addressed.

Wilco came into being after the demise the alternative country band Uncle Tupelo led to singer Jay Farrar quitting after repeated clashes with Tweedy to form Son Volt. Tweedy retained the rest of the band and named them Wilco after the abbreviation used in the military and aviation services used for the response "will comply" a sense of humour and heavy irony was indicated from the outset.

They cut *A.M,* an album which was overshadowed by the Son Volt debut and followed it with *Being There* named after the Peter Sellers film - a double album for the price of a single on the understanding they would forgo their part of the profit. The album sold well costing them a fortune but Tweedy felt it was all worthwhile. Next came the joint album with Billy Bragg *Mermaid Avenue* which found musical settings for Woody Guthrie's late period lyrics he had been unable to perform in the grip of the emphysema that killed him. Recording was extremely strained as Wilco and Bragg had completely different ideas how the material should be treated, nonetheless the album was released to a fine reception and healthy sales.

Amid all this Tweedy was experiencing marital difficulties and his absence from his wife and son while touring was weighing heavily upon him as was an addiction to painkillers. With this as the backdrop Wilco, or rather Tweedy and multi-instrumentalist

Jay Bennet, entered the studio to record what would become *Summerteeth* leaving the rhythm section of John Stirratt and Ken Comer very marginal roles in proceedings. Tweedy took his marital problems and laid them bare, framed in a prose style influenced by the amount of twentieth century literature he was reading. Whilst using Pro Tools, he and Bennet constructed mostly piano-led tracks filled by inventive use of mellotron and synthesizer. Stirratt was quoted as comparing the record to, *A Heart Of Darkness*. The record company weren't happy but agreed to release the record if a track *("I Can't Stand It")* be remixed for single release. This was agreed as 'a one time only' deal.

To me the closest precedent and spiritual cousin to Summerteeth would be *Big Star's* third album where they too went down to a duo and experimented freely in the studio. The difference is where the *Big Star* record was ramshackle, Summerteeth is beautifully honed and full of Beatlesque melodies, a Phil Spector-like sound and a Brian Wilson-like gift for harmonies that conspire to disarm the listener – for underneath this glorious Technicolor pop veneer voices whisper malevolent and disturbing messages such as "I dreamt of killing you last night – it felt alright to me" a particularly vivid insight from the spellbinding *"Via Chicago",* an utterly deranged melodrama placed in the very centre of the album. Two songs later *"My Darling"* is sensitive and sweet suggesting the emotional storm clouds have passed, but have they?

This was the turning point record for Wilco, this was where Jeff Tweedy truly found a voice to go along with his undoubted melodic gifts, this was where the studio began to be used as an instrument in itself and in that sense it is the key record in the career of a fascinating band opening the door to a fearless, uncompromising approach to the art of making music.

13. Pulp
We Love Life
(2001)

Pulp were part of the big three of Brit-pop, not quite having the mass appeal of either Blur or Oasis but always being way more cool than either of those. They were seen as wacky and colourful, releasing songs that resonated with their hedonistic audience whilst simultaneously making them smile with their sly humour.

Pulp were never quite what they seemed however and their humour was often the conduit for real anger. They sang about night-life and good times but always through the prism of the next day's hangover and disappointment at how shallow and unfulfilling all they'd dreamed about turned out to be in the cold light of day; relationships, glamour and fame itself all ultimately had the capacity to extract any joy from their souls leaving them darkly depressed and picking at the scab in a pit of existential squalid thoughts.

They were the band who people who disdained Brit-pop could still like but the trouble with fashion is it's fickle and if you're ever 'in' you can bet your life soon enough you'll be 'out' and that is where Pulp found themselves by the time they came to record this album.

There had been a three-year gap since the previous release of *This Is Hardcore,* a vicious swirling vortex of a record, had signified in no uncertain terms that the party was over. It was not what was wanted by their audience and was soon gracing CD section bargain bins. But where that album has in the intervening years been resurrected and reassessed and is now viewed as the band's 'left-field classic' *"We love life"* came and went with little fanfare and has almost been airbrushed from history, ironic because it is perhaps the best album of their career.

After aborting sessions with Chris Thomas, the reins were picked up by Scott Walker which proved an inspired choice. The album at once sounds more organic than Pulp had sounded in a long time. The chirpy synths that underpinned much of their best-known work are replaced with swells of backing vocals from the Swingle Singers and both acoustic and electric guitars and supple bass feature prominently. There is a bucolic flavour of nature that runs through the album but it is a countryside of weeds and tangled sharp thorns and brambles. The other motif is death, *"Roadkill"* and *"The Night Where Minnie Timperley Died"* are the most explicit examples. Where Minnie "A girl who has sex with teenage wrecks, waiting for her DJ brother who's lost his decks" accepts a lift that presumably ends in her murder. There are two spoken word pieces that are brooding and highly effective among the conventional songs that all create a more sombre mature mood than on previous works. The lyrics are more direct and pared back compared to what we are accustomed to from Jarvis Cocker, his mocking tone replaced by a more reflective wistfulness.

The centrepiece of the album is *"Wickerman"* where underneath the city runs an underground river that ebbs and flows hidden from the populace at large, elsewhere *"Bad Cover Version"* concludes that a past lover has simply replaced real love with a pale imitation and even finds time to have a dig at side two of producer Scott Walker's *"The Band Played On"* album before the album concludes with *"Sunrise"* but even there the feel is uncomfortable as if after a long sleepless night the light is harsh and painful on the eyes.

The band called time on their partnership not long after the release of this album that managed a chart run of just three weeks. If you blinked and missed it at the time may I humbly suggest this is a great album waiting to be rediscovered and loved.

14. David Bowie

Let's Dance (1983)

For three and a half decades until he shuffled from this mortal coil, each David Bowie release would at some stage be hailed as his best since the nineteen eighties *Scary Monsters And Super Creeps* which is rather telling in how critically maligned the album's follow up, *Let's Dance,* had become.

Very strange too that this musical icon's biggest-selling album became regarded as an artistic aberration, if not quite the turkey the two follow-ups were judged to be and indisputably were. *"Let's Dance"* was the template they followed and so it grew to be disdained and unloved.

In the three years between *Scary Monsters* and *Let's Dance,* Bowie had zig-zagged from one disparate venture to the next. He'd taken the role of John Merrick in the Broadway production of Elephant Man, collaborated with Queen on the huge hit *"Under Pressure",* acted on a TV play *"Baal"* which spawned a fascinating five-track EP and worked with Giorgio Moroder on the title music for a quite pathetic cinematic disaster *"Cat People".* The song Bowie and Moroder recorded for the opening credits was so good it almost redeemed the rest of the sorry mess. These varied projects suggested Bowie's creative mind was far from dormant and rejuvenating the team around him was par for the course to prevent staleness creeping in.

So trusted producer/ lieutenant Tony Visconti was jettisoned for Nile Rogers, at the time the go-to guy for rockers looking for some added funk. Also out was long-time guitar player Carlos Alomar who was replaced in an inspired move by up and coming Texas blues wizard Stevie Ray Vaughan. The album was cut in just seventeen days, Bowie knowing full well he was at his best working hard and fast, one or two takes per track and trusting his instinct but not only was the album a huge commercial success but to my ears it is absolutely essential as well.

It is bright sounding, with lots of space for the songs to breathe. Lyrically it was much more spare than *Scary Monsters* had been but compared with the minimalist approach utilised on *Low,* for instance, it sounded positively florid. A strangulated chugging guitar riff opens the album that is reminiscent of Jimi Hendrix as drums and piano take us into *"Modern Love",* which bobs and weaves as a saxophone snakes around the beat. *"China Girl"* is given a stunning makeover from the version Bowie and Iggy Pop had recorded for the latter's *"Idiot"* album five years previously. Gone is the claustrophobic paranoia of the original version replaced by an altogether lighter, breezier reading that if not surpassing the original is certainly its equal. The title track follows and released as a single, became an enduring monster hit; its shuffle beat, parping sax and the joyous crescendos of the chorus refrain mark it as one of those special moments in a career littered with special moments. *"Without You"* follows and indeed followed the first three album cuts in being released as a single, though it was too understated to court much in the way of chart action it was a fine track. Still to come were *"Ricochet"* and a remade *"Cat People"* that, though fine, suffered in comparison with the original version. A cover of *Metro's* *"Wonderful Criminal World"* displaying Bowie's knack up to that point for judicious choices in the material he borrowed. Before this remarkable though often maligned album finished in fine style with *"Shake It"* which seemed to marry a Devo-style rhythm with Brides of Funkenstein-like backing vocals and Bowie back in *"Young Americans"* vocal territory absolutely nailing a wonderful vocal.

Tastemakers may disagree but if prejudices can be set aside I think many would find much to love here at the start of Bowie's written-off decade.

15. Basement Jaxx
Rooty (2001)

Felix Buxton and Simon Ratcliffe could be stood next to us at a bus stop and despite the fact that they produced a house soundtrack of uplifting genius to enhance our lives we wouldn't know. They are largely invisible, the cover star of this album 'Snowflake the albino gorilla' would be far more recognisable than either Buxton or Ratcliffe. That level of invisibility and lack of image has worked against Basement Jaxx being afforded the respect they deserve.

Where their contemporaries, Daft Punk, Air and even the Chemical Brothers all project a public face that helps an audience to feel a connection with the artist and draw attention to the brand, Basement Jaxx lack that unifying ingredient in their records and may as well be by myriad performers for all the brand loyalty they inspire.

Because of this and the fact that their records are so much fun that they feel like guilty pleasures to hipsters who need either authenticity or to be in on the joke - Basement Jaxx seem so blatant that they are often deemed 'cheesy', the ultimate hipster insult. All of which ignores the magnificence of the records released by this duo, particularly in their early years when ideas seemed to tumble from them. On this, their second album, the sound is raw and vibrant and no matter how long was taken tooling up the grooves on this record, there is no lack of immediacy – it is brash and in your face, like a funfair taking place on a discotheque dance floor.

Pitchfork's review described the record, "...Often so tacky it's impossible to stomach", *Pop Matters* conclude that, "...Either a brilliantly innovative record, or an unlistenable mess, depending on your point of view." I find it vibrant and uplifting in the way in the same way that only those who don't care about appearing to be cool are better company and seem blessed with purer spirits.

Five UK hit singles were the yield from this album of which *"Romeo"* and the adrenaline charged *"Where's Your Head At"* were among the decade's finest. The hippest cats on the block might well have never ventured near this but that is quite simply their loss.

16. Love
Four Sail (1969)

"Never let the truth get in the way of the myth" is an oft-heard statement that tends to rub me up the wrong way, it provides a hiding place for liars and charlatans and writes inconvenient truths out of history. Give me the reality everyday, I don't want romantic notions; I want facts, I want truth.

One of the big Rock & Roll myths concerns Love. It is that quite simply they recorded three great albums, culminating in the baroque masterpiece that was *Forever Changes* and then, having burned up all their creativity and inspiration, band leader Arthur Lee sacked the band and never released any worthwhile music again as he succumbed to madness haunted by demons that took him to the very brink before he was granted a reprieve and came back to remind the world how great *Forever Changes* was before taking a final bow and shuffling off this mortal coil.

The truth is though that the album Lee released as the follow-up to *Forever Changes* was in itself a quite stunning album and even though it slipped through the cracks into relative obscurity should not be dismissed, that album was *Four Sail*.

The *Forever Changes* band had fallen to pieces. Bryan Maclean, the writer of some of the group's best known material, elected to quit and pursued the dream of solo success to little avail and Lee found himself at the helm of a listing ship crewed by heroin addicts. He lined them up to walk the plank and recruited a new band. There was an immediate change of sound and musical direction. Gone were the beautifully adorned folk trappings to be replaced by a harder blues guitar-led re-imagining.

The album starts off with an echo of the past in some glorious flamenco style playing as of yore before veering off into a hard-hitting dramatic riff with new guitarist Jay Donnellan given plenty of room to shine. That is followed by *"Your Friend and Mine"*, a bitter-sweet lament to Love roadie, Neil Rappaport, who had apparently sold the band's equipment for drugs which precipitated a death by overdose. Musically it's a saccharine sweet concoction which goes some way to disguising the acidity of the song's sentiments. Also of note was side one's closer, *"Singing Cowboy"* which concerned itself with a gunslinger haunted by the ghosts of his unfortunate victims.

Side two opens with *"Dream"*, one of the greatest songs Arthur Lee ever wrote and one where he writes in the first person, displaying an emotional honesty not often revealed. *"Robert Montgomery"* follows and is another classic superbly constructed and performed. *"Nothing"* is a spiritual soul-searching Meditation and quite exquisite. "*Talking In My Sleep*" lightens the tone a little before the album's highest peak is reached on the closing "*Always See Your Face*", featuring a muted French horn and a beautiful arrangement that harks back to previous work.

It is a quite superb album that has been overlooked for far too long and which I've held in my heart since first hearing it in the early Seventies courtesy of my brother's exemplary taste.

17. Pink Grease
This Is For Real (2004)

A few singles and a gloriously trashy EP paved the way before *Pink Grease* unleashed their debut album to practically no response whatsoever.

They found themselves completely out of step with what was going on in the wider world where earnestness was the watchword. *Pink Grease* paraded garish charity shop glam. Their manifesto seemed to be to party as hard as humanly possible until lipstick was smeared like a repulsive scar, mascara was streaked, skin was pallid, eyes were red and raw and the smell of stale alcohol, cigarettes and sex at least overpowered the stench of vomit.

This Is For Real may have been the album title but. "...is it for real?" was the question on the critic's lips we had regressed to the state we had been in when a previous generation's journalist taste makers had sneered at *Roxy Music* for their supposed inauthenticity whilst ignoring the blindingly obvious genius of the band and their oblique statements. That's not saying *Pink Grease* were the new *Roxy Music*, they most certainly were not! Where the latter, even at their most experimental, seemed possessed of chic and glamour, *Pink Grease* embraced the trashy garish reality of dole queue living, city dwelling, creative types marginalised by the mainstream who were channelling their art through vibrant noise.

Vibrant and noisy is indeed a good description of this album – it has all the subtlety of a sledgehammer. It is a fizzing concoction of big guitar riffs, blaring horns, squelching home-made synths and electronic devices with singer Rory imploring, squealing and yelping through the lyrics. The Punk glam references were obvious and inevitably trotted out as the band were compared to T. Rex,

The Damned, David Bowie and The Rezillos but although those comparisons are valid and undeniable, I also hear some of the high intensity Hip Hop as served up by Public Enemy in the brew. There's also the disco groove of Giorgio Moroder and the fevered passion of MC5, in fact a real rag tag grabbing and plundering of a kaleidoscope of influence.

I truly love this record; its aim was never to change the world but nonetheless captured a time and a place and reflected the world around it by its rejection of the "you can't do that" ethos of the harsh working class landscape that was capable of crushing spirits. Pink Grease were indeed for real and to paraphrase another bunch of shouty sloganeering noisemakers from a previous generation they were having "a riot of their own".

18. Barry White

Stone Gon' (1973)

What is it that confers cool on Isaac Hayes' brand of symphonic soul; his albums highly prized collector's items, while the similar sounding Barry White is regarded as something of a joke figure? His supposedly cheesy and inconsequential music is in fact highly sophisticated and atmospheric but his albums are the staples of junk shops and car boot sales.

Perhaps it's simply the unbelievable level of success White enjoyed that decades later still causes resentment that lead to a lack of appreciation for an amazing talent, decades after his heyday and years after his death.

What's for sure is that Isaac Hayes, Al Green, Curtis Mayfield, Marvin Gaye, in fact all the titanic figures of Seventies Soul music would have given their right arms to have had the knack that White had; writing, arranging, producing and performing an endless stream of classics that the public on both sides of the Atlantic flocked to buy. Barry White was no joke and those who consider him to be are either cloth-eared, delusional or suffering from a bad case of musical snobbery.

White was initially a reluctant performer who seemed happier in the background but on hearing a demo meant to showcase his songs, music business mogul Larry Nunes convinced White to re-record them and issue them under his own name; his first album containing his first hit, *"I'm Gonna Love You Just A Little More Baby"*. An emboldened White re-entered the studio to record *Stone Gon'* his second album which is a near flawless joy.

I'm not going to try to describe Barry White's sound because if you're reading this I'll presume you've heard him. It was said if chocolate fudge cake could sing, it would sound like Barry White and that's a good enough analogy for me. *"Honey Please Can't Ya See"* and *"Never, Never Gonna Give You Up"* were huge chart singles extracted from this album. They dominated the airwaves and the dance floors in equal measure, to the extent I'm transferred back through time on hearing the opening bars of *"Girl It's True, Yes I'll Always Love You"*. He should also be placed on a pedestal as a performance to aspire to, so sincere does White sound throughout the combination of blissed out strings and horns, creating a warmth while beneath it the rhythm doesn't falter, as wah-wah guitars almost sing and the unhurried languid growl and purr of White's voice conspire to create a very special album indeed.

19. Bob Dylan
Self Portrait (1970)

Four years before Lou Reed issued *Metal Machine Music* presumably to wipe the slate clean of the Lou Reed image in a move that confused and then angered his record company, the critics and a large chunk of his audience, Bob Dylan had done precisely the same thing with this sprawling double album loaded with cover versions and badly recorded tracks from his appearance at the Isle of Wight festival. He was of course trying to kill off 'Dylan' the mythological "spokesman for a generation". What a drag that must have become for him, how was he supposed to live up to the expectations of the masses of crackpots who hung on his every word attaching deep significance to every syllable and believing *"Blowing In The Wind"* or *"Masters Of War"* would change the world. It was all too much and Dylan was going to prove to them he was only a human being, not some messiah for the 'Woodstock Generation'.

So much for gestures and the personal politics of the piece but was it any good? The critical consensus at the time was that it was not. Everyone from radio DJs to the most influential rock critics from the largest selling magazines queued up to kick the album, denouncing it as an act of betrayal and an insult to his audience to the extent that this view was accepted as the fact of the matter by the populace at large. One of the few dissenters was a then unknown Marc Bolan who felt compelled to write a letter to the press opposing this view.

It would take *Blood On The Tracks* and *Desire* to re-establish Dylan's reputation before once again he wilfully tore up the script with a pair of gospel albums and an Eighties catalogue that was always defiantly true to the artiste's muse but troubling for his audience. But back to the matter at hand; *Self Portrait* was always a much better record than has been credited – for sure the quality of the material and the performances vary wildly and often the overdubbed backing singers and strings are clumsy and unnecessary but like the Beatles' *White Album* and the Clash triple set *Sandinista* the abrupt changes in mood and quality of recording keep the listener attentive and involved.

The album starts with the two line *"All The Tired Horses"* sung by female backing vocalists 'the voice of his generation' pointedly absent before Dylan appears on his own *"Alberta"* which was pretty much a rewrite of *"Baby Let Me Follow You Down"* which he'd covered a decade before on his debut album. The covers here range from an atrocious but funny take of Paul Simon's *"The Boxer"* to brilliant readings of *"Copper Kettle"*, *"It Hurts Me Too"* and *"Days of '49"* while of the originals, the beautifully crooned *"Living The Blues"* and *"Quinn The Eskimo"* show Dylan in fine form and enjoying himself.

Self Portrait was a declaration of personal independence and a "fuck you" aimed at those who wished to use his music for their own agendas, but it's also an enigmatic document of where a great artist was at as the Sixties dream withered and it's a splendid quietly riotous record too.

20. Lindisfarne

Nicely Out Of Tune (1970)

Although nowadays pretty much regarded as passé, those of us with long memories can conjure in our minds a Lindisfarne who weren't lame Geordie cheerleaders with fixed grins resembling denim-clad father figures for Ant and Dec to smugly emulate but a band of refreshing casual brilliance. Unassuming and working class, they promised much but only delivered fleetingly before their fire was doused by internal politics and disagreements.

Lindisfarne appeared to be a tight fellowship bonded by real camaraderie, but the truth is they were a disparate bunch who shared little in common apart from their place of birth. They had come together out of the ashes of several local outfits only months before this album was begun in 1969; which is perhaps why it is special and far and away their best work as they enjoyed a honeymoon period where there was a sense of cooperation that couldn't last. Perhaps also another piece in the puzzle of why this album was so superior to what followed was the cheapness of its recording. As newcomers they were not afforded much of a budget and put into an antiquated eight-track studio when twenty-eight track was the norm. The relative crudity of the equipment means the performances have an immediacy and striking sparseness that gave way to a fuller less appealing sound on their next two albums.

The album opens with *"Lady Eleanor"*, a Gothic Edwardian tale of love and mystery that rides along on a mesmerising, wholly effective mandolin part. *"Road To Kingdom Come"* follows in rocking style and is such a contrast to the opening track it's difficult to equate as being from the same band. Yet part of what made Lindisfarne so special was that though ostensibly a 'Folk Rock' band, that categorisation was far too small to encompass all the directions they shot off into. The third track *"Winter Song"* is a quiet meditation on inequality and the iniquity of poverty, Alan Hull working two jobs trying to raise a young family champions the downtrodden in what is a simply brilliant piece. Other stand-outs include *"Clear White Light"* a song from a confirmed atheist that concerns itself with the search for faith and answers to unanswerable questions; it is a beautiful shimmering piece.

Side two opens with *"We Can Swing Together"* which became a sing in unison concert staple and looks at how the law seems to come down heavier on some rather than others. *"Alan In The River With Flowers"* a titular parody of the Beatles' *"Lucy In The Sky With Diamonds"* is a confusing, seemingly paranoiac piece blessed with a quite sublime melody. The album tails off with the rather silly *"Down"* before *"The Things I Should Have Said"*, an understated wistful lament, restores the quality only to fall away on a pointless run through in square dance style of Woody Guthrie's *"Jackhammer Blues"* and then a rather self-pitying but elegant *"Scarecrow Song"* plays out this remarkable album.

21. The Groundhogs
Split (1971)

As the realisation dawned that the Sixties dream was over and bands looked for a way forward, many jumped onto the Blues as a way of channelling their oeuvre. The trouble was that 99% of said bands were clueless imposters with no feel for what they were playing which conspired to draw attention to how horribly contrived they were, right down to the phoney Mississippi delta accents they used. They aimed for authenticity inauthentically, it was cultural appropriation at its most ludicrous.

Groundhogs could easily have been tempted into following this preposterous path but thankfully, despite being named after a John Lee Hooker song and backing many touring Blues legends during the Sixties boom, they remained as English as fish and chips.

Their previous album *Thank Christ For The Bomb* had made huge commercial inroads, reaching the British top ten with songs concerning the horrors of war and previous to that, I kid you not, the band had a number one single in Lebanon but *Split* would be the most successful of their records, going top five.

While never changing the perception of them as a 'freak band', this album lyrically and musically took inspiration from a panic attack endured by song-writing, guitar playing head honcho Tony 'TS' McPhee which from opening phrase, "from the dying embers of a burned out day", set to a circular riff, the whole episode is played out in four parts. McPhee was a thrilling unshowy master of wrangling noise from the guitar, Ken Pustelnik absolutely thrashes his drum kit and Peter Cruikshanks' bass throbs and pulses throughout. This was a powerhouse trio but they never lost sight of the dynamics that make this album a marvel. We move through the four stages of *Split;* McPhee's Jack Bruce-like voice at the centre of the maelstrom and flip the record to find side two's opener *"Cherry Red"* simmering for a couple of seconds before its pulverising riff thunders out of the traps.

Split is a captivating wild stomp that saw the band appear sadly for the only time on the BBC's *Top Of The Pops,* no doubt to head scratching and a small level of consternation from the family audience. *"A Year In The Life"* inspired by the similarly named Beatles track, slows everything down before the band hit the deranged sounding *"Junkman"*; McPhee railing against the trend towards processed food that would soon become an avalanche, noise dredged rather than conjured up fills the track sounding like a creature in pain clawing to the surface from deep underground before giving way to the final track *"Groundhog",* a slide guitar shuffling tribute to John Lee Hooker.

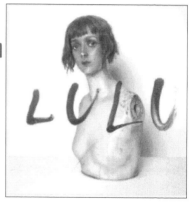

22. Lou Reed & Metallica
Lulu (2011)

At the turn of the 20th century Frank Wedekind had written and staged *"The Lulu Plays"* that concerned a young dancing girl who employed her sexual wiles to advance her position in society before being plunged into an abyss of poverty, violence and prostitution. It challenged, nay, in fact affronted the moral codes of the age, pushing through the barriers of what was permissible subject matter for art.

That Lou Reed was attracted to this work was hardly a surprise with his love of the dark hearted tales of Edgar Alan Poe and the grit of Hubert Selby Jr's *"Last Exit To Brooklyn"*. The hidden repressed underbelly of society was often where Lou had cast his eye for inspiration, so *Lulu* was a gift waiting for him.

Lou and Metallica had performed on the same bill at Neil Young's *Bridge* concert in 2009 and an alliance had been discussed. Now here was the opportunity; Lou recognising that to make this record an artistic success, to make this record meaningful, it would have to be brutally hard, absolutely unyielding, not an ounce of compromise could be countenanced or the integrity of the piece would be polluted. He had nothing to lose, having burned his bridges with a mass audience as far back as 1974 with the ultimate 'fuck you' gesture that was *Metal Machine Music* - nobody could doubt his sheer bloody mindedness or underestimate his willingness to offend again. For Metallica it was a different proposition, although still the undisputedly biggest 'heavy' band on the planet, they had wobbled in the eyes of their audience by using acoustic guitars on their previous album; how would this bunch of notoriously straight-jacketed ultra-conservatives cope with an album fronted by 'Grumpy Lou' the godfather of Punk? They had a lot to lose but credit to them, they didn't flinch when the album was released to a barrage of abuse from critics and audience alike. Lou Reed received death threats for what he had done and no doubt he laughed long and loud at the reaction.

The double album is everything the critics describe; monolithic, pulverising, lacking humour, relentlessly gloomy and visceral but where they perceive these things as negative, I would suggest they are what make the record a complete triumph. Lou described it as "The best stuff done by anyone ever" and I don't believe he was joking because as far as he was concerned he'd made precisely the album he'd dreamed of making. It was a triumph and was described as "more Lou Reed than Lou Reed himself" which is no bad thing to my mind. Through each track Lou spits venom unconcerned by melody, what little of that there is comes by way of James Hetfield's backing vocals accompanied by a barrage of Brutalist noise from the band. Track after track drags you deeper into an unforgiving emotional black hole, it was all recorded live, face to face, wound up and tense; Reed at one point challenged Lars Ulrich to a street fight.

We don't hear that, but there is tension aplenty and a tangible undercurrent of violence. It is a powerfully unpretty and unapologetic album where singling out individual tracks is a pointless exercise. Each piece belongs to the whole and that is the way to digest and understand this monumental work best; crank it up loud, let it hit you, let it purge. There is not an ounce of flab on this record. It is a punishing, astonishing piece of work that defies convention, not some simpering apologetic background noise that would go down nicely with dessert. Almost begging to be loved, this was Lou at his challenging uncompromising best, taking no prisoners.

23. Van Der Graaf Generator

Godbluff (1975)

Beloved of a tiny devoted (largely male) audience Van der Graaf tend to be lumped into a category labelled "Prog Rock" alongside Yes, Pink Floyd, and Genesis when in truth they were a truly autonomous unit who shared none of the orthodoxy of their peers.

For them there was not the slightest prospect of mainstream success, they were far too awkward a proposition for that. They barely used the guitar, preferring avant Jazz flourishes played on sax and flute. The organ was used heavily but not in the same way Rick Wakeman or Keith Emerson used it as an instrument of bombastic macho excess but in a studiously anti-Rock way. Even the drums had a lightness and restraint to them and playful passages added a disarming gentleness on occasion only for a maelstrom to follow hot on the heels. Of course the most striking instrument in Van Der Graaf's armoury was the strident edge of a cliff intensity of vocalist Peter Hammill.

On this album Van Der Graaf were returning after a four-year absence, a split that was never complete because in the intervening period between the band's last release *Pawn Hearts* and this return, Hammill had pursued solo projects which often incorporated his three former band mates, yet on this return there was a noticeable difference to their sound. For the first time self-produced, they were tighter, starker and stripped of some of their tendencies to wander. Studio experimentation gave the material an immediacy and drama like never before. This is the Van Der Graaf album where the debt owed by John Lydon and Mark Smith is most obvious, indeed The Fall went as far as to parody the cover for the release of their own 2005 *Fall Heads Roll.*

The album contains four tracks of almost equal length beginning with *"The Undercover Man"* which starts quietly on a bed of flute and drum before organ and steering vocals fill the soundscape. Next *"Scorched Earth"* changes tempo at a remarkable rate and Hammill acts out the disturbing (aren't they all?) lyrics going from a whisper to wolverine howl. The chaotic, angry *"Arrow"* starts side two and is a powerful, passionate, disturbing, nightmarish song, "How strange my body feels impaled on this arrow", Hammill cries in anguish. The album concludes with *"The Sleepwalkers",* a long daring piece that incorporates elements of Music Hall and Bossa Nova in its musical detours around the central elements of the song where Hammill uses every vocal inflection in his extensive repertoire to express the strangeness and internalised fear of the sleepwalking man.

Van Der Graaf were deliberately designed to be too difficult a proposition for general acceptance and divide opinions too much to have ever been hip, but for anyone who requires adventure as part of their musical diet they are an absolute necessity.

24. Slade

Alive! (1972)

Nineteen seventy-one was a big year for Slade; following the release of two flop albums and a disastrous flirtation with a Skinhead image, it was hard to take them seriously, let alone anticipate their imminent success. But they played live constantly, honing themselves into an act who knew how to pace a gig and knew how to play a crowd. Early in the year *"Get Down And Get With It"*, a raucous slice of Rock & Roll, put them into the charts. Another single, *"Hear Me Calling"*, a cover of a Ten Years After track was cut but rejected before the violin led *"Coz I Luv You"* took them to chart nirvana in October 1971. Simultaneous to this, the thorny question of what to do about the next album was being addressed. Much seemed to be riding on it or the band could easily have been perceived as a flash in the pan - the pressure was on to get it right. The decision was made to attempt to capture the magic of the band in a live setting and three nights were recorded at London's six hundred capacity Command Theatre Studio; it proved to be an inspired choice.

The album crackles with atmosphere and only three original songs are spread across it and two of those had appeared on the previous albums. These tracks are sandwiched between cover versions to which the band attached their own stamp. The good time atmosphere is apparent from the moment the needle hits the groove and the power is turned on for a crackling assault on the aforementioned *"Hear Me Calling"* followed by their own equally hard and fast *"In Like A Shot From My Gun"* the band are clearly having a good time and sound solid and very confident as they slip into John Sebastian's poignant and tender *"Darling Be Home Soon"* that features the moment when Slade's 'people's yobs' reputation was secured as a well-oiled Noddy Holder belches into the microphone during a quiet interlude before the band run through the gears into a roaring crescendo. *"Know Who You Are"* is a swaggering punchy call to arms whilst *"Keep On Rocking"* and *"Get Down And Get With It"* play the crowd for all they're worth. While *"Born To Be Wild"*, the classic anthem of American bikers, is transported to the A-roads of the UK retaining all its defiance and power.

It was mission accomplished for Slade, the album was released following another big hit - the Lennon-like "*Luck Wot U Dun*" and went to number one making them, along with T. Rex, the biggest band in the country. A much loved people's band who made great singles, although never another great album, Slade were sneered at for being far too popular, colourful and parochial to be considered cool. At best they remained a guilty pleasure for the serious rock brigade and were largely dismissed as 'teeny-bopper fodder' and massively underrated but *Slade Alive!* remains one of the best live albums in an era of great live albums and is worthy of a place in any record collection.

BRYAN
FERRY

25. Bryan Ferry

These Foolish Things (1973)

Bryan Ferry pastiched the lounge lizard Lothario so well that in no time at all the join between the real and imaginary became invisible and the work of art that Ferry sent out to promote his musical endeavour became revered for his elegance and chic.

A style icon imitated by weekend hedonists and aspiring pop stars alike, he was the epitome of cool and the fact that the bitter longhairs of the music press sniped at his lack of authenticity, dubbing him "Byron Ferrari", only emphasised the gulf that was widening between the Sixties throwbacks and those at the cusp of the sea change that was the Seventies.

Bryan Ferry was at the forefront of fashion and seemed untouchable in his position of preening prominence, but of course the downside of fashionability is that it inevitably changes and what was 'in' yesterday is 'out ' tomorrow. Sadly, Bryan Ferry these days has become an anachronism, mocked for his political views, for his affiliation with the aristocracy, and most of all mocked for his music which is derided as sterile and lacking in emotion. What is odd about this judgment is his work with *Roxy Music* is untainted by these criticisms and rightfully applauded for its daring; they remain untouchable.

Ferry was busy in 1973; Roxy released *For Your Pleasure* at the beginning of the year, he sacked Eno, replaced him with Eddie Jobson and the newly configured band recorded and released *Stranded* at the year's end. In-between came his first foray as a solo artiste, *These Foolish Things* was an album of cover versions that has become a junk shop staple but is an absolute gem of a record.

The 'sainted' Bob Dylan's Cuban missile crisis commentary, *"A*

Hard Rain's A Gonna Fall" is the opening track and was a major hit single but Ferry takes this serious piece of work and turns it into a glorious, unforgettable romp. Never had Dylan's song craft been treated with such a lack of respect, but freed from the baggage of its message its playful heart was revealed. The same treatment is afforded each song, the mission seems to be to locate the pop heart of each piece and display both the serious songs, *"Sympathy For The Devil"*, *"You Won't See Me"* and the supposedly banal confections, *"Baby I Don't Care"*, *"It's My Party"* and show them as equals when stripped of the artifice draped over them.

The final song and title track of the album *"These Foolish Things"*, harks back to the pre-Rock & Roll era and seems to be a deliberately positioned coda to what has preceded it and a gentle statement that all these foolish things are simply songs we can enjoy if prejudicial thinking is not allowed to dictate what is considered to be cool.

26. Diana Ross
Diana (1980)

Diana Ross's previous album, the Joe Perry produced *The Boss,* had both satisfied her followers and been a hit, but there was a feeling that her records were becoming short on the fun factor. The effervescence of her Supremes recordings and those from her earliest solo sides had been sacrificed in the process of repositioning her as an icon rather than simply a pop star. To address the issue, Bernard Edwards and Nile Rogers were brought in to write and produce an album that would bring the fun back into a Diana album.

It was an inspired choice and indeed an inspired pairing. Rogers and Edwards' own band Chic were at once hugely successful, highly respected and on a creative hot streak and not content to rest on their laurels, they were workaholics. In 1980 alone they wrote and produced a Chic album, one each for Sheila B Devotion and Sister Sledge, as well as this. All were excellent but this was the one with the cherry on the top.

Songs were written after conversations with Diana to ascertain what exactly she wanted and to make sure they were 'singing from the same sheet'. At one point she reputedly stated she wanted to 'turn everything upside down and have fun', inspiring the writers to conjure the spirit of *Studio 54* and write and arrange *"Upside Down"* and *"Have Fun (Again)"*. Elsewhere the gay anthem *"I'm Coming Out"* was inspired by the number of New York drag queens who used Diana as an inspiration for their look. The record sounds like it was fun to make and a reinvigorated Diana performs stupendously, her voice rich in character, she effortlessly puts her individual stamp on proceedings even though the patented Chic Organisation sound is as distinctive as it is alluring. Rooted in traditional R&B but recalibrated to make them the most forward thinking studio practitioners of the era, the combination of their expertise and talent with Diana's voice and star power was a perfect match, but still problems arose when Diana and Motown got distinctly cold feet.

The recording was deemed too radical. Amid America's Disco backlash they feared Diana's career was at risk if this music was issued as it was and so without Edwards' and Rogers' knowledge or consent, they returned to the studio, remixing and editing, speeding up parts and adding new vocals to create a commercially more palatable version of the album. It was issued without any single released from it which was most unusual for a Motown album and indicates how unsure about this album the executives were. But radio DJs picked up on *"Upside Down"* and when given a single release it became a huge and enduring hit.

The album became a massive seller, the biggest of Diana's career, and despite the complications elevated the reputations of Edwards and Nile ever further. *Diana* is an enduring classic of an album without a weak track. There are jubilant celebratory moments, particularly *"I'm Coming Out"* but more reflective emotional fare such as *"Now That You're Gone"*. I'll admit that it's not a record that enhances street credibility but it is one capable of lifting sagging spirits and putting a twinkle back in tired eyes.

27. Saturday Night Fever Soundtrack

(1977)

1977 is widely regarded as the year that Punk broke out of squalid clubs and dirty venues and landed, kicking, screaming and spitting, in the living rooms of the middle-aged and comfortably off. Watch a TV retrospective of that year and *Anarchy* is perceived to have been everywhere and the music scene was dominated by spiky-haired youths shouting over a three-chord thrash. Or at least that is the accepted version of the year HM Queen celebrated her Silver Jubilee and the Sex Pistols got a sneering single to the top of the charts in the same week.

In reality of course there was a lot more happening than Punk. This was also the golden age of Roots Reggae, although the fact that it has come to be seen as little more than an adjunct to Punk seems a tad racist as well as patronising. Then there was the enormous commercial and artistic success of Fleetwood Mac and their album *Rumours* which took up residence in every mortgage holder's record collection in '77.

To taste-makers, Disco exists purely as a naff soundtrack for badly dressed people's Saturday nights, when in reality it truly ruled 1977. This record, and the film from which it was extracted, were fundamental in bringing the sound of New York gay clubs into the mainstream of British and American life and the musical landscape was never quite the same again.

The Bee Gees were in France recording a new album when label boss Robert Stigwood asked if they could help with songs for a low budget movie he was financing called *"Tribal Rites of a Saturday Night"* after the record company bosses' first choice,

Boz Scraggs, had vetoed the use of his material. More out of loyalty to Stigwood than any faith in the project, The Bee Gees acquiesced and submitted *"If I Can't Have You"*, *"Night Fever"* and *"More Than A Woman"*, while another song *"Saturday Night"* was altered because of the preponderance of songs with the same title to become *"Stayin' Alive"*. The previously recorded *"Jive Talkin'"* and *"You Should Be Dancing"* added to the score. With Yvonne Elliman performing *"If I Can't Have You"* and Tavares *"More Than A Woman"*, alongside contributions from Trammps, MFSB and KC And The Sunshine Band plus quasi-classical pieces written by the film's musical director David Shire acting as bridges between songs, this was an album of pure dynamite starring The Bee Gees alternating between downright funky and lovelorn balladeers with groove.

Singles were plucked from the album that dominated that year's charts and the album itself sat at the top of the pile for an eternity. It's never easy to retain a 'cool' disposition when it has to exist alongside 'omnipotents'. *Saturday Night Fever* didn't manage that feat but don't let that diminish the fact that this album was an absolute triumph, it was glorious and celebratory, as well as being of the highest quality. That it is an era defining-record can brook no argument, and that's pretty cool.

28. The Mekons

The Curse Of The Mekons (1991)

Of all the bands from the class of 1977 and the Punk Uprising, none has been so uncompromising in their stance as oppositional voices against the injustices inflicted upon the weak by the powerful, none have doffed the cap less in pursuit of fame and fortune while repeatedly jabbing at the soft underbelly of the Rock & Roll industry than The Mekons. They have trod their own path and produced stunning music along the way, easily a match for mega-selling peers such as Elvis Costello or The Clash and for their troubles they have seen exposure and audiences dwindle to a hardcore of devotees as year by year they grew ever more unfashionable.

I state categorically, as someone who was privileged to watch a lot of Mekons shows from the mid-eighties into the early nineties, that there was not a band on the planet to touch them. They had the tunes, they had the intelligence, they had the passion and there was nothing throwaway in their music. They were riotous fun and quite simply the best party in town.

This album followed the A&M records released *Rock & Roll* which was a magnificent record that sold minuscule 'units'. A&M refused to release this follow-up meaning it was unavailable in the USA for a decade. Thankfully Blast First issued it in the UK. There are more quiet songs featured here than on previous albums often sung beautifully by Sally Timms. *"Waltz"* and *"Wild & Blue"* are superb but topped by *"Brutal"* which follows the drug trail taking in the Chinese Opium Wars and CIA trafficking. The rough-hewn voices of Jon Langford and Tom Greenhalgh roar and croon alternately and never without complete conviction as Langford states incredulously, "This funeral is for the wrong corpse" and asks "how can something really be dead when it hasn't even happened?" as the demise of Socialism was celebrated by the ever-encroaching capitalist tide of the Nineties, while Greenhalgh warns "The abyss is close to home" repeatedly on *"Sorcerer"*, a track built on a cyclical groove which is made more dramatic by the falsetto voice employed throughout.

Sonically *The Curse Of The Mekons* takes in echoes of Reggae, Country and the Avant-garde while a huge array of instruments including banjo, violin, bagpipes and synthesiser all feature prominently and never sound out of place alongside the regular tools of guitars and drums. They all combine wonderfully and add colour to the material creating a mournful atmosphere undercut by a quiet but steely defiance to continue the resistance and not to let hope be extinguished.

29. The Style Council

Introducing The Style Council (1983)

This was the eagerly-awaited debut from the outfit Paul Weller put together after The Jam had called it quits at the height of their career. That band had been lumbered with far too much baggage for any mere mortal to carry while their limitations musically meant the focus would always remain narrow. Weller, infatuated with the idea of Modernism, felt stifled in a rock three-piece and felt compelled to move on without the ball and chain of audience expectation shackling him. It was a brave move in an industry where playing safe is the norm, it was also flirting with career suicide especially when the Parka-bedecked hordes heard the music.

Many felt betrayed and offended by this record. Where there would have been acceptance for a music harking back to the golden age of Sixties Soul, what was offered up was shiny and contemporary. Many wouldn't get past the first track *"Long Hot Summer"* which languidly floats along on a groove and a lush bed of sound borrowed from post-disco popsters Imagination.

Weller had never sounded better. He was full to the brim with ideas he could express from the songs to the pretentiousness of the sleeve notes written under his alias 'The Cappuccino Kid'. There followed the more up-tempo *"Speak Like A Child"* a deserving big hit single. His sidekick, ex-Dexy's and Merton Parkas man Mick Talbot, weighed in with the Ramsey Lewis-like *"Mick's Up"* and the album concludes with *"Money Go Round"* a clattering slice of up-tempo funk and polemic riding on stabbing guitar, propulsive bass and drums, swelling organ and thrilling horns not dissimilar to

Spandau Ballet's excursions into similar territory; it was Beggar and co style-wise but with a lot more substance.

The Style Council were neither loved or cherished. They were given little respect either, regarded as an indulgence too far. The records they released are regarded as dispensable when measured against those by The Jam and Weller's later solo years. I'd contend that this is the best record of his career and The Style Council years were his most artistically fruitful. To quote Robert Wyatt, "The wilderness is a very underestimated place, and sometimes the most important moments of what you do are when you sidestep the main road".

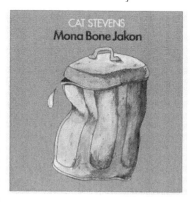

30. Cat Stevens

Mona Bone Jakon (1970)

In 1967, the teenage Cat Stevens became a pop star, riding high in the charts *with "I Love My Dog"*, *"I'm Gonna Get Me A Gun"* and *"Matthew And Son"*. His first album replicated that success and, as is the way of things, in those days a second album was required shortly after and expected to yield another harvest of hits. It was recorded, released and fell flat on its face despite containing *"The First Cut Is The Deepest"* which was later to become a hit for multiple artists. The audience had simply moved onto something new. It was a chastening experience for young Cat and then, at his lowest ebb, he contracted tuberculosis which hospitalised him and necessitated a twelve-month recovery period during which much thinking was done and a set of songs written much different in tone than those that had made him a star.

The result was *Mona Bone Jakon* which the singer revealed as being his pet name for his penis! It was a much more minimal record than was expected. Out went the heavily orchestrated Chamber Pop of yore to be replaced by acoustic guitar and piano with unobtrusive percussion while the songs themselves, though sketchy, retained the melodic flair of their creator but were laced with questioning, streaked with pessimism and often referencing death. It was a record remarkably adult in its themes for a twenty-year-old. Scott Walker wasn't the only Sixties teen heartthrob making the transition towards being regarded as a serious artist.

Track number one, *"Lady D'Arbanville"*, played as a madrigal, was darkly mysterious and when plucked from the album became a hit single. *"Pop Star"* laid out Stevens scorning the triviality of stardom. Three of the tracks; *"Trouble"*, *"I Wish I Wish"* and *"I Think I See The Light"* were used in the brilliant black comedy

"Harold and Maude" and helped Stevens become re-assimilated in the public consciousness.

His distinctive, older than his years, lived-in voice did the rest to make him the bedsit troubadour of choice for a generation of sensitive souls. Huge success followed but this, alongside follow up *Tea For The Tillerman,* remain his finest albums. Somewhere along the way his music lost its spark, simplicity and beauty. Cat became Yusuf Islam and disappeared largely from the public eye to follow a different path as his music unjustly fell out of fashion and favour.

31. Konono N°1
Congotronics (2004)

There was a period in the mid-Eighties when the term 'World Music' was coined, Womad flourished and *The Indestructible Beat Of Soweto* album shipped a massive amount of units.

Names were dropped, artists toured and the multi-faceted music of many African nations seemed set to follow Reggae out of the Third World ghetto and into the hearts and homes of the affluent West. Hipsters appropriated the garb and talked the talk, but then as Acid House and Grunge happened they dropped African adornments in favour of smiley faces and hoodies or plaid shirts and oversized boots.

That has been pretty much that and only occasionally in the years since has an African act ignited interest and attention before limited attention spans mean they invariably end up neglected and almost forgotten. One such act who briefly illuminated the music scene during their fifteen minutes of fame were Konono N°1 particularly with this album, *Congotronics*.

Based around the likembé thumb piano, traditional street musicians in the Congolese capital Kinshasa, under band leader Mingiedi Mawangu's Bazombo ethnic group, soon discovered they needed amplification to compete against the hubbub of street noise. They say necessity is the mother of invention and it was certainly the case here as scrap car parts and magnets were used to create an ad-hoc sound system which, when switched on, created a huge swelling hum that was incorporated into the music. The music however is based on centuries-old pieces from pre-electronic days transformed by the alignment of this surging power aligned to the percussion played on pots and pans, the whistles and chanted vocals into avant garde expression that is utterly unique.

What emerges is a joyous celebratory trance dance that is hugely hypnotic and not comparable to any recognisable western sound. This is a once heard, never forgotten album that sounds incredibly live, although it was supposedly captured in a studio, although audience applause seems to suggest that is a falsehood. Tracks often start simply enough before becoming more multi-textured with complex intertwining rhythms that intoxicate as well as fascinate. Taken individually any of the tracks are monstrous dance-floor fare but as a whole the album is a writhing snake-like creation of repeated peaks, it is an absolute triumph.

32. Argent

Encore (Live in Concert) (1974)

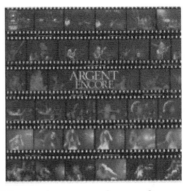

Argent were a band I'd go and see often in my mid-teens. I really liked them and they always put on a good show plus tickets (even in an era when all concert tickets were cheap) were very cheap and despite this incentive their gigs never sold out, there was plenty of room. It must have been very dispiriting for them but I confess I liked the fact that the masses didn't like Argent, it meant I didn't have to share the pleasure I got from their records and shows with people who only liked the current big thing.

Argent belonged to a select few and I was one of them and, as I congratulated myself on my own good taste, I was as smug as could be! That was my teenage logic and I misguidedly believed the band would be perfectly happy with this state of affairs. They got to make records and some were even minor hits, while they toured regularly in an era when travelling extensively was the preserve of only the 'elite' bands. I didn't realise that they'd have liked to have been as successful as Pink Floyd or Yes, I assumed it was enough to just be better than them which they were but no, it wasn't enough.

Argent had been formed from the ashes of The Zombies who had been much loved, leaving them constantly fighting to escape unfavourable comparisons as they tried to establish themselves. *"Hold Your Head Up"* had been a biggish hit, *"Tragedy"* and *"God Gave Rock and Roll To You"* minor ones, but they didn't sell the quantities of albums to be elevated towards the premier acts of the day.

Pressure had built up and by the time this staple of Seventies rock, the live double album, was released, Russ Ballard, front man and composer of 50% of the bands repertoire, had left the band but this proved to be perhaps their best and most consistent record devoid of much in the way of filler material and showcasing the band in a way where the fault line between Russ Ballard's Rock & Roll sensibility and Rod Argent's more grandiose inclinations was clearly audible. It may have been problematic to the band but it added tension and dynamics to the mix as the earthy and the highbrow battled for supremacy; Ballard's choppy guitar riffs against Argent's neo-classical keyboards with the solid as a rock rhythm section of Jim Rodford and Bob Henrit holding steady. Two writing styles to contend with, two which in truth proved an asset in the sense there was always light and shade on offer to the listener, though one can only guess at how much each band member felt compromised by the other's style.

The album opens, it has to be acknowledged, catastrophically with the Rod Argent (and writing partner and ex-Zombie Chris White) penned *"The Coming Of Kohoutek"* which is frankly a shapeless mess, but picks up with Ballard's *"It's Only Money Parts 1 and 2"* and, *"God Gave Rock & Roll To You"* displaying the pop sensibility the band always retained. "Thunder and Lightning" shows a harder rocking approach, *"Dance Of Ages"* is stately, *"I Don't Believe In Miracles"*; delicate and *"Keep On Rolling"*; a barrel-house piano stomp before an elongated *"Hold Your Head Up"* that never loses its focus leads into *"Time Of The Season"*, a song impossible to dislike, and that was that the end of the show and the end of Argent as we'd known them, though they soldiered on with two new recruits unsuccessfully attempting to fill Ballard's shoes.

They were never a big success, never fashionable or remotely hip but Argent deserved more than they received and are worthy of revisiting.

33. Electric Light Orchestra
Eldorado (1974)

The high concept of ELO had collapsed almost as soon as it had begun. Roy Wood, intent on making music where the strings were integral, as opposed to Jeff Lynne's more pragmatic vision of traditional rock songs with strings adorning them, quit dissatisfied and disappointed after an Italian tour where the string players' contributions were rendered inaudible by the amplification, to form his avant-rock and roll ensemble Wizzard.

Many expected ELO to bite the dust as the perception was that it was very much of Wood's conception. Add to the fact that Wood was an acknowledged pop genius where Lynne was regarded at the time of being of lesser pedigree but the latter persevered and over the next couple of years his knack of conjuring up hit singles kept the band afloat. Still, clouds remained overhead as this, the band's fourth album, was being written. Lynne's father had criticised his son's music as lacking melody. Lynne took that point on board and clearly sought inspiration from his Beatles LPs - this album would be remarkably Beatlesque. He also wrote out a storyboard for the loose concept the album would follow concerning a man who escapes his tedious reality by living in a world of daydreams. However the most telling decision was the hiring of a thirty-piece orchestra to participate in the sessions rather than grafting on cello and violin to finished tracks almost as an afterthought. The effect was dramatic, creating huge rich swells further enhanced by the presence of a choir lifting the music to previously unimaginable heights.

The album opens grandly with *"The Eldorado Overture"* which plays like a grand Hollywood theme promising magic and adventure before giving way to *"Can't Get It Out Of My Head"* probably Lynne's finest composition, yearning and gorgeous, in fact quite sublime. *"Boy Blue"* too was a delicious concoction. Track one on side two is *"Mister Kingdom"* echoing *"Across The Universe"* although it was nonetheless beautiful and the frenzied *"Eldorado Finale"* feels as if one is sat in the centre of the orchestra pit as it spins around your head.

Legendary avant-garde LA filmmaker Kenneth Anger went on to use the album to soundtrack the re-release of his 1954 film *"Inauguration Of The Pleasure Dome"* which is a fine indicator of the record's luminous cinematic quality. In the USA the single *"Can't Get It Out Of My Head"* gave the band their first hit and propelled the album to gold status within weeks, making ELO a highly viable and lucrative proposition. In the UK, neither single nor album charted, although over the next few years huge sales would be achieved for the band, yet in their homeland despite that success they would always find themselves sniped at, regarded as trivial; a novelty band who squares loved. It's an attitude that persists to the present day, but it shouldn't. This album was a triumph from start to finish. The band would never come close to emulating it in terms of artistic quality, an open mind is all that's required to enjoy and appreciate this classic.

34. The Vibrators
Pure Mania (1977)

To be regarded as a 'punk fake' in 1977 was to be rendered completely uncool; once a band or individual was tainted by the allegation, a palpable unpleasant odour was forever attached to them.

That The Vibrators were indeed 'punk fakes' and 'bandwagon jumping imposters' is an undeniable fact. They were too old and had all been around the block several times before the arrival of the Sex Pistols which heralded the coming of multiple acts chopping their hair, narrowing their trousers and speeding up songs - all topped off with a trademark sneer.

For The Vibrators, bassist Pat Collier had even served time as vocalist for The Ray Coniff Orchestra beloved of mums, dads and grandparents. Credit the band though with being quick out of the blocks, they played a John Peel session as early as October 1976 and were amongst the first of the new groups to release a single. Still The Vibrators were vilified whereas the likes of The Jam, The Stranglers, The Drones and Slaughter and the Dogs were given a much gentler ribbing for similar crimes against 'Street Credibility'.

Pure Mania was released in June of the 'Summer Of Hate' and for the growing legion of less puritanical followers of the new Punk thing, it was manna from heaven. For all their lack of credibility, The Vibrators viewed simply as purveyors of a sound rather than a socio-political instrument of insurrection, were prime exponents of tuneful sing-along Pop Punk played well and given a crystal clear production gleam. In fact, listening to this record devoid now of the baggage of the time, one becomes aware what a little nugget of pop gold this album is.

Lead singer Knox and bassist Pat Collier proved themselves

adapt tunesmiths with a knack for catchy choruses and guitarist John Ellis was a cut above the majority of his peers in his tasteful utilisation of sounds to colour the basic meat and two veg structures of the songs and on occasion unleashed demented angular shards of noise solos that elevate the band beyond the chugging mass that were attempting something similar.

Nothing is as up-tempo as one might expect; the Ramones/ Clash emphasis on speed is eschewed for a more Pistols like medium pace attack, 'into the future', 'keep it clean' and the mildly risqué 'whips and furs' are all winners. The song *"Stiff Little Fingers"* gifted a bunch of teenage Ulster boys a band name and *"Baby Baby"* dropped the BPM to a snail's pace and was very sweet indeed though not quite sweet enough to chart when issued as a single.

The Mania may well have been contrived rather than pure but what was served up is as good a slice of guitar pop this side of Blondie's emergence from Bowery Bar to world domination.

35. Wings
Wildlife (1971)

When considering the merits of any work by an ex-Beatle, one cannot escape the context of the piece. There was no escaping the long shadow of their shared past for any of them and they all referenced it in song on their subsequent records. Everything they did retained the subtext of ex-Beatle, they would never be judged solely on their own merits, so deep had the parent group penetrated our collective psyche. Paul was perceived (along with Yoko) as the villain of the piece and there was a backlash of negative vitriol aimed at his work, even *Ram* which preceded this record (a work of staggering musical invention) was savaged by the critics as lightweight and unworthy of his legacy.

Now they grumbled he had the audacity to form a new group! Unthinkable, unbelievable and unbearable for those clinging to the notion that their beloved mop-tops might yet bury the hatchet and reunite, this was the final nail in the coffin for that kind of wishful thinking as John Lennon rather than Paul had said, "the dream is over".

In August 1971 Paul and Linda McCartney, drummer Denny Siwell and ex-Moody Blue, Denny Laine, became Wings after barely being introduced to each other and were almost immediately whisked into the studio to record this album inside a week. This was not going to sound like The Beatles, in fact this was not going to sound much like anyone or anything else. Songs were jammed and improvised, they are often tentative as the musicians strive to find common ground, but throughout there is a fun vibe transmitting from vinyl to listener. The sound is spare, uncomplicated and intimate. Those few of us who fell in love with the record found it an absolute revelation, demystifying the apparatus that surrounds stars. For others, *Rolling Stone* magazine captured the majority opinion describing it as, "flaccid, impotent, trivial and unaffecting". They were listening through cloth ears, they were writing spiteful bile driven by their own agendas and values which were being challenged by the striking boldness of this record, its quiet understatedness throwing a gauntlet down against the prevailing ethos of the day.

The record begins with "*Mumbo*", a thrilling made-up-on-the-spot rocker with a groove and spontaneous nonsense lyrics which is followed by another infectious piece of glorious meaningless fluff that none the less makes you smile, "*Bip Bop*" before fifties-sounding hit "*Love Is Strange*" is given an effective reggae makeover years before Eric Clapton made a hit of, "*I Shot The Sheriff*" or The Clash enhanced their Rebel Rocker status by covering "*Police and Thieves*". Side one then concludes with one of Paul's patented Little Richard like raw emotional rockers.

Side two is more orthodox containing 'proper' songs but "*I Am Your Singer'* is wonderful for Paul coaxing the non-professional Linda to the mic to duet with him, it's heartfelt and sincere, saving the best to last is "*Dear Friend*" one of those rare occasions where Paul unburdens himself in a lyric addressing his relationship with John Lennon, this olive branch would be answered a few months later by the icy blast of "*How Do You Sleep?*" when Lennon's overproduced and somewhat sugary *Imagine* album was released.

Thumbs aloft, stoned, stupid, plum-coloured hair Paul might just be the most uncool man in music this side of Cliff Richard or Demis Roussos but the man has proved time and again he is a musical genius and *Wildlife* is, I promise, a superb album that suffered for being unconventional and decades ahead of its time.

36. MC 900 ft. Jesus with DJ Zero

Hell With The Lid Off (1990)

This is one of my favourite albums that knocked me for six upon release. This lovingly took the form of a Hip-Hop album while simultaneously being nothing of the sort. The sarcastic and very pointed lyrics take pops at charlatans of many guises from evangelical preachers to seemingly wholesome family entertainers yet it never follows the rhyming flow of Rap but comes across as beat poetry. Its mumbled, shouted, sometimes heavily electronically treated and sometimes stated naked and confidently. Musically, although heavily scratched and laden with samples, this owes little to Hip Hop but is a kind of playful imaginative amalgam of Jazz and experimental Electronica.

MC 900 ft Jesus was the name chosen by Mark Griffin, previously of Texan post-punk outfit The Telefones, after watching a TV evangelist claim to have been visited by a 900 foot Jesus who commanded him to build a hospital. DJ Zero was one Patrick Rollins who certainly deserved his equal billing displaying an innovative style all of his own to create a soundscape at once complimentary to the lyrics as they roll without regard to conventional structure. Though nothing here would fill a dancefloor, it has you nodding your head and pleasantly twitching even during the darkest creepiest moments which come thick and fast.

The most recognisable song is *"Truth Is Out Of Style"* which delights in lampooning Shirley Maclaine as a figurehead of all that is perceived as good in American entertainment. *"Talking To The Spirits"* incorporates African chants and rhythms with the vocals buried in the murk reminiscent of Dr John's epic track *"Angola"* and like it concerned with the power of satanic symbols in our society. *"I'm Going Straight To Heaven"* is pure funky joy with DJ Zero pulling out all the stops utilising a horn sample as an infectious punctuation mark. The record veers from that to *"Spaceman"*, a floating Jazz piece with cocktail piano adorning it while MC 900 ft Jesus slowly tells a tale that incorporates a spaceman collecting waste cans to be turned into currency before noting that Europe is getting smaller as he floats away into the infinite.

It really is a wonderful strong piece of fully formed work, dark-hearted but cheerfully poking its tongue out at the hysterical scaremongers who profit from instilling fear into people's minds. A true classic then but impossible to bracket and therefore impossible to market, meaning this album is remembered fondly only by the few... but oh my goodness it is excellent and I must say the live performances in support of the album took the thing to an altogether higher level than anything we're likely to see anytime soon.

37. The Stylistics

The Stylistics (1971)

As the Seventies began, social and cultural change was everywhere; it was a time for new beginnings. In America the Vietnam War split the country across generations and no amount of moon landings could halt the tide of criticism in art, film and music. Marvin Gaye issued *What's Going On?* while Sly And The Family Stone put out *There's A Riot Going On* - both were brilliant Soul records that belonged to a new decade that critiqued government policy. It may surprise some people who picture the Stylistics as the ruffle-shirted perma-smiling embodiment of bland production lined AOR sweet soul to realise that they were in on the act too with a finger on the pulse on this their debut album.

"People Make The World Go Round" was six-and-a-half minutes of socially conscious protest wrapped up within beautiful shimmering vocals, lush strings and the expertise of musicians who would soon become known as MFSB, the lynch-pins of "The Sound Of Philadelphia". *"Country Living"* advocated a back-to-basics approach to combat the failed capitalist system.

In truth, the Stylistics themselves had no say in the direction their material took them. Their record label had ceded all artistic control to Thom Bell who had just been hugely successful with The Delfonics. Initially reluctant to work with The Stylistics, Bell found himself won over by the remarkable pure falsetto voice of lead singer Russell Thompkins Jr whose sense of timing enabled Bell to construct dramatic showpieces of the highest quality around him.

This album contained five American hits within its nine tracks including *"Stop Look (Listen To Your Heart)"*, *"Betcha By Golly Wow"* and *"You Are Everything"* all recognised to this day as classics and if the up-tempo *"Point Of No Return"* had been released as a single it may well have earned the same kind of status. Over a three year period that yielded three albums, the combination of The Stylistics, Thom Bell, his writing partner Linda Creed and the musicians and producers at Sigma Sound released faultless music that raised the bar in terms of sophistication for all who wished to emulate this glorious sound.

Bizarrely, the band's greatest European success came in their post Thom Bell years with more garish and much inferior recordings but let's ignore those here and celebrate this landmark of American Soul Music.

38. 10cc
Sheet Music (1974)

I recall vividly the ill-conceived Buxton festivals of the early Seventies contained some great bands; the likes of The Faces, Chuck Berry, Mott The Hoople and Humble Pie all rolled up to entertain the soaking, shivering throng on unlovely, unsheltered bleak moorland. It was a scene Hieronymus Bosch might well have conjured up if transported through time and space, it was truly hellish.

I still chuckle though when I replay one incident in my mind - DJ John Peel, who was clearly more open minded than his audience, had the temerity to play "*Silly Love*" from this album, the response was immediate and furious, the affronted longhairs rolled around in the mud scooping up filth to hurl at a quite empty stage while trying to drown out the amplified music with whistles and booing. It was a strange time when university educated white musicians sought authenticity by pretending to be black Blues players from the Mississippi Delta. No wonder they hated 10cc, a band who completely rejected this artifice and instead played snappy, intelligent and very English Pop while looking (in the context of the times) very ordinary, quite boring in fact; they were stiffs, not hip to the scene but more to the point their lack of cool left them sorely underestimated and under appreciated.

Sheet Music is the second 10cc album and it represents the band at their absolute peak as a fully functioning self-contained cooperative unit made of four unique and distinct talents who, in combination, became a creative juggernaut emboldened to experiment inside a studio they had built in Stockport far away from the prying eyes of Tin Pan Alley.

The band operated as two distinct writing teams: the oddball and artful Kevin Godley and Lol Creme and the crafted classicist pair of Graham Gouldman and Eric Stewart. But at this time there was enough respect between them for this arrangement to be fluid in the extreme and so some of the wilfulness of the former was tempered by the latter, while on the other hand the former were allowed to inject some madcap moments into the orthodox work of the latter, each complimenting and strengthening the other.

Beginning with "*Wall Street Shuffle*", a pointed rebuke aimed at heartless financiers who would "sell their mothers because they can buy another", the fun begins... next up is the inexplicable flop single "*Worst Band In The World*", which pokes fun at the Rock & Roll myths concluding that the bottom line is all about shifting units, "my plastic turns to gold". "*Old Wild Men*", is a lament for the "old men of rock & roll"; the Sixties heroes who'd become bland and complacent, while "*Clockwork Creep*" is a song about a time-bomb on an aeroplane. So far, so eclectic as they flit effortlessly between styles and with four very capable and distinctive lead singers, nothing is predictable.

Side two rides in on the helter-skelter guitar figure of "*Silly Love*", "*Somewhere In Hollywood*" is aching but arch simultaneously whereas "*Baron Samedi*" is a Saturday morning matinee-style romp before "*The Sacro-Iliac*" leads us through a new dance and finally "*Oh Effendi*" promises "still more goodies in the pipeline" to end one of the great unsung albums - a record rich in invention, beautiful in conception and hugely entertaining.

39. Win

...Uh! Tears Baby (1987)

Davy Henderson's Post-Punk outfit The Fire Engines had worn their funk-loving hearts on their sleeves throughout their tenure as cult heroes to a faithful few, with ideas much bigger than their record sales and music that deserved a wider audience. The inevitable came to pass and The Fire Engines were retired and Win were birthed and re-tooled for an unapologetic tilt at mainstream success.

1985 saw the release of a pair of independently released singles before almost by default they ended up as part of the London Records roster, unchampioned and unloved within that organisation it would be a brief unhappy marriage but none the less 1987 saw this, the release of the first of Win's two outstanding albums.

The game plan seemed to be to align cryptic, smart lyrics with the effervescent pop melodies the gifted Henderson plucked seemingly from thin air. Add insanely over-the-top vocal arrangements that suggest Busby Berkeley musicals and a glossy state-of-the-art production sheen to create a sweet appealing soufflé of sound so intoxicating it would sell by the shed load.

Musically the album is similar in its use of a synthesised backdrop to that of ABC or Heaven 17 with the spectre of Prince, Bowie and the glam stylings of Marc Bolan evident. Opening with what could be a manifesto of sorts "Super Popoid Groove" fizzes like sherbet, incorporates a riff so epic it could have come from a Big Country hit, contains a cheerful sing-a-long chorus and enough peaks to constitute a whole mountain range as it teeters between madness and genius; it is perfect pop.

A repeating piano figure underpins "Shampoo Tears" giving it a vaguely Northern Soul feel. "Un American Broadcasting" dips into The Fire Engines back catalogue retaining the brittle funk emphasised by a stark piano motif and the chanted chorus but adds a rich velvet coating. Flipped over, the record starts with "Empty Holsters" which alternates between a creeping verse and a huge chorus that is vaguely Christmassy and quite sinister. "You've Got The Power" is one of those hits that never was, despite being issued thrice as a single and used on a much televised advertisement for lager, it is a mystery how a track so catchy and optimistic didn't break the band into the chart act where they aspired to and deserved to be.

Each track is laden with hooks, choruses positively boom and it's a quick-witted record that can be sung along to, danced to or simply listened to and enjoyed. On its release "Uh! Tears Baby" hit number 51 in the charts, it was there for a week before disappearing and becoming largely forgotten.

40. Cockney Rebel
The Psychomodo (1974)

Declaring war on post-Woodstock hippy excess, Cockney Rebel was launched as a defiant anti-lead guitar alternative to the screeching but saying nothing formula that dominated the music scene.

Described by the New Musical Express as "Mincing Biba dummies" long before the dawn of the Sex Pistols, Steve Harley had that publication nailed as the 'eNeME'. The *NME* rejoiced at the failure of first single "Sebastian" and the album The Human Menagerie, sniping with accusations of hype and the suggestion that Cockney Rebel were no more than a talentless Roxy Music clone. In early 1974 though, the charts were breached by stand alone single *"Judy Teen"* laying the groundwork for this album that followed three months later and was propelled into the top ten by kids sensing this was truly something different.

A tour was quickly undertaken where resentments felt by the musicians toward their autocratic leader led to a mass exodus leaving only Harley and drummer Stewart Elliot to pick up the pieces. Their success had lasted mere weeks. Harley would put together a new Cockney Rebel as a backing band and this new version, though more orthodox, was far less inspirational but would assist Harley to the stardom he craved before his talent was squandered and ebbed away in a quest to broaden his appeal and Cockney Rebel became no more than a, for the most part, forgotten relic – a sad fate for a band who stoked the embers of rebellion from which punk would rise and who left behind this masterpiece as their epitaph.

Few albums start so audaciously and in such unorthodox fashion as *Psychomodo*. What sounds like a ship sinking (The Titanic) gives way to sawing violin and a lyric that is a gossamer-veiled attack on the band's critics "Pop paper people printing Rebel insane!" before clattering to an abrupt halt mid drum beat and launching into *"Psychomodo"*; all fractured shards of angst and disgust delivered in a sneering whine over jaunty keyboards, chattering drums and riffing violin "Destroy!" Harley states, "I wish I could die" nailing the nihilism of the blank generation three years early. *"Mr Soft"*, the album's hit, is excellent but such is the quality elsewhere on the album it feels like a lesser song.

Still to come are the killer tracks *"Ritz"*, a shimmering trip through a tainted paradise which finds Harley at his most poetic and abstract lyrically suggesting dislocation and feverish visions. "Cavaliers" is full of defiance and drama "I'll spit in your eye, it's better than lying anytime" but delivered by a wounded man awaiting his inevitable fate, it's a track to a journey that winds inevitably toward a heart of darkness. And finally to the last track of the album, *"Tumbling Down"* an audacious graceful lament in which half-remembered half-imagined losses are laid forth until the music lurches into an enormous refrain of, "oh dear look what they've done to the blues" with Harley, by now rasping and straining, screaming the words at his backward-looking musical peers.

Their star didn't burn brightly for very long and what little respect they earned was given grudgingly but for this one album alone Cockney Rebel deserve to be loved.

41. Poet And The Roots

Dread Beat an' Blood (1978)

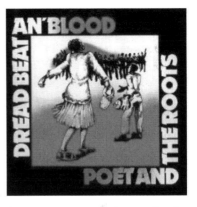

British Reggae and record poetry both receive sour-faced expressions if mentioned in polite society and yet this album by 'Poet' Linton Kwesi Johnson and The Roots, who were the cream of the British Reggae scene, helmed by producer Dennis Bovell, is as powerful a document now as it was in the late Seventies, telling tales of the oppression and outright racism encountered by Black Britons at the hands of our institutions.

The anger is measured, the voice never hysterical, the descriptions of events and depictions of mistreatment ring true and are harrowing. The music constructed to frame the words are full of empathy; heavy and serious but never morbid.

We are taken on a trip into the inner cities of police stop and search tactics (the infamous 'Sus' laws) and back of the van beatings. We hear of the murder by racists of George Lindo in *"Dread inna Inglan"* while the prescient, *"All Wi Doin Is Defendin"* foretells of the riots that would come three years later as youths armed with bricks and bottles fought back against the injustices that occurred on a daily basis.

This was an album where LKJ shone a spotlight on an area of society invisible to the masses but which was an inescapable everyday occurrence for the black communities of the inner city; a truth of casual racism that denied them opportunities in employment and education, where police harassment was off the scale as they abused their powers. This was a powerful indictment of a racist state creating an ethnic underclass that was marginalised and distrustful. LKJ leads the fight back not with violence but with reason, intelligence and a passionate, authentic voice.

"Man Free" demands the freeing of Darcus Howe, the black academic and civil rights campaigner jailed for three months for assault after being set upon on the London Underground. All these stories tell us what our society was truly like in the 1970s, they are lessons that still need to be learned.

In his relentless monotone, Linton Kwesi Johnson's voice over Roots Reggae made us listen and made us think, this album is a treasure to be passed down as our unwritten history in Dub.

42. ABBA

Voulez-Vous (1979)

ABBA are admired nowadays, having proved their ability to craft a prolific number of memorable pop gems at such a prodigious rate during the mid-to-late 1970s that it beggars belief. Yet that admiration often falls short of outright love as ABBA are often patronised by trendy types just as they were in their seventies heyday. It's only pop after all…

ABBA the Album and its spin off film *Abba the Movie* had proved to be enormously successful, dominating the charts of 1976 but by 1978 Abba were experiencing something of a creative block. Days spent working in the studio were producing not a note of usable material and tensions were mounting that would later shatter their personal relationships, A single, *"Summer Night City",* was released despite major reservations from the band members as to its worth. It performed dismally for an ABBA single, reaching only number five on the charts! It was a disaster for this consummate singles act. They were searching for a spark of inspiration and found it in a rented apartment in the Bahamas to which Benny and Björn decamped in order to expose themselves to American music that was not transmitted on the conservative Stockholm airwaves. When the *Saturday Night Fever* soundtrack album began yielding hit after hit for The Bee Gees, they listened to Earth Wind and Fire's alignment of melodies and groove and found their new direction. ABBA set about making a disco album, even laying down the backing track to the title song in the Miami studio used by the Gibb brothers.

From start to finish the album took a year to make but it sounds remarkably fresh and alive. The vocals have a warmth and vitality. The Swedish musicians used regularly on ABBA's records deserve as much acclaim as the LA based Wrecking Crew or Motown's mighty Funk Brothers – they were absolutely impeccable and play with real fluidity. And of course the songs, while never going to win awards for literature, are mini-masterpieces, hook-laden and memorable.

The disco makeover fit ABBA like a glove too and helped transform them into gay club icons, although two of the albums biggest hits *"Chiquitita"* and *"I Have A Dream"* were both cut from the Euro-pop cloth that had built the band's reputation. The title track alongside *"Angel Eyes"* was a huge hit as was *"Does Your Mother Know"*. Not even included on the album was *"Gimme Gimme Gimme'* which became a hit a few months later which indicates the quality of this album that contained no filler whatsoever.

43. The Carpenters
A Song For You (1972)

By the time this, the fourth Carpenters album, hit the racks, dorky brother and sister duo Karen and Richard were being described as "A perfect embodiment of American youth" by none other than nefarious slime ball President Richard Nixon. Unsurprisingly, like most of Nixon's utterances, it was a comment that proved to be absolutely miles away from the reality.

Though their airbrushed public image showed no imperfection, the blissed-out smiles for the cameras hid painful truths. The Carpenters were on a phenomenally successful run as hit followed hit. Their previous albums seemed to be simply thrown together to meet deadlines with little regard for the creation of a substantial piece of work. They were scatter-gun affairs with low points as numerous as high points. This album addressed that problem and for anyone interested in the music of the Carpenters beyond their numerous greatest hits anthologies, this record will give the most pleasure and satisfaction. It is without doubt the best album of their career displaying the full range of their talents. Richard was a superb writer and arranger while Karen had a voice that contained genuine warmth and a range of expressiveness that marked her as one of the greatest singers in the history of recorded music.

The album yielded no less than six hit singles, very much the currency of the day but these were not simply ephemeral pieces of pop fluff but enduring classics such as *"Goodbye To Love"* with its soaring fuzz guitar solo that saw it boycotted by the more conservative American radio stations and launched the era of the 'power ballad', a version of Carole King's *"It's Going To Take Some Time"* is the definitive take of the song. *"Hurting Each Other"*, *"I Won't Last A Day Without You"* and *"Bless the Beasts and Children"* match those for quality and there is still *"Top Of The World"* to be mentioned. Even Richard's pair of solos showcase the instrumental *"Flat Baroque"* and the jaunty *"Piano Picker"* work extremely well in the context of the album, adding a change of mood and variety.

The Carpenters never matched the quality of this album but then that quality is extremely high and within a decade Karen was dead. Her death and the manner of it led to a re-evaluation of the Carpenters legacy and briefly they became a name to drop in chic bohemian circles. Some of the appreciation was doubtless sincere but much of it was to do with the ghoulish iconography attached to the tragic early death of a celebrated figure. Karen and the music she made with her brother are worthy of much more than that.

44. Pearls Before Swine

One Nation Underground (1967)

I once knew a deeply troubled individual prone to psychotic episodes who was dangerous to himself and anyone in the vicinity. He was no stranger to the mental health services and the police. There came a point when he vowed to put a stop to the modes of behaviour that contributed to his problems and he visibly cleaned up his act, becoming noticeably tidier and swearing off alcohol and drugs as he attempted to introduce order into his chaotic life. One final symbolic act remained before he could fully embrace his rebirth and so with much ceremony he took his copy of this album and hurled it into the river freeing himself from the sickly pervasive influence it had exerted on his life.

Whether he succeeded in finding the peace and contentment he sought, I don't know. He simply disappeared leaving no clue as to where he had gone. I tell this tale to illustrate how much is read into this album, what tricks it plays and what significant power is attributed to it by the tiny but rabid band of acolytes it has affected.

Pearls Before Swine were named after a passage in Matthew 7:6 in Jesus's Sermon on the Mount: "Do not give what is holy to the dogs; nor cast your pearls before swine, lest they trample them under their feet, and turn and tear you in pieces". They were led by singer-songwriter Tom Rapp and found a home with esoteric New York label ESP Disc after noting that the similarly outre Fugs recorded for them. Primarily a psychedelic folk band, they also incorporated elements of Garage Punk into their hard-edged sound. This may have been the summer of love but these freaks were the antithesis of flower power and the beautiful people. They created something extreme, something black-hearted and at times ugly; a potent swirling mix suggesting a very bad hallucinogenic trip in the company of a fire and brimstone Old Testament preacher.

They mix mysticism with a guttersnipe's viewpoint as if Donovan had been a member of The Velvet Underground. *"Another Time"* played acoustically describes a lisping Rapp walking unscathed from a car crash. *"Uncle John"* on the other hand is angry and spiky, while controversy was the result of *"(Oh Dear) Miss Morse"* when it was realised that the word FUCK was spelt out gleefully in morse code as the jaunty tune is played on banjo and stabbed organ.

Packaged in a sleeve featuring the Hieronymus Bosch painting "The Garden Of Earthly Delights" everything about this record is perfectly realised conceptually, it is atmospheric and mysterious but too strangely unsettling to have ever been embraced by the masses or be regarded as cool.

45. Jerry Lee Lewis
Live At The Star Club, Hamburg
(1964)

Rock & Roll holds little in the way of cool in the Twenty-First century. There is little reverence afforded the artists of that era although their forebears, the Blues players of the Southern Delta and urban Chicago, are held in high esteem so it certainly isn't just a case of the mists of time obscuring the brilliance contained in the cream of that genre. Jerry Lee Lewis was possessed of rare brilliance, a superb performer who practically reinvented the way the piano was played and a singer whose unconventional style managed to convey something feral and contemptuous in a society that had condemned him and the people he knew to dirt-poor lives and harshness in the rural south.

Jerry Lee had, through a combination of his raw talent and sheer bloody mindedness, become a Fifties star releasing some of the most ferocious records of the day only to see his career crash against the rocks in the scandal that followed news of his marriage to his thirteen year-old cousin Myra. Jerry Lee was defiant and unrepentant but extremely embittered as well. This wild man became wilder, more cussed and more volatile and although his recording career was seemingly over he played night after night in small clubs honing his craft until his edge was so sharp it could draw blood.

This album was recorded cheaply in 1964 when to the world at large Rock & Roll was dead, swept away by the beat groups who followed The Beatles. If anybody had informed Jerry Lee of this fact he hadn't paid them any heed and no concessions were being made to changing fashions. Using British act The Nashville Teens as a backing band, Jerry produces a performance that is primal and brutal. There are no peaks and troughs, just one set-long peak from beginning to end. The intensity of the performance is relentless as he whoops and hollers and sounds as if he is attacking the piano keys with a hammer so hard are they being hit.

"Mean Woman Blues" is no gentle opener to warm up the crowd, it goes straight for the throat. Jerry sounds like a man possessed - it is exhilarating to hear such a naked and pure performer letting loose his demons. How he maintains the excitement as he runs through *"Money"* and *"Matchbox"* is incredible and by the times he hits *"What'd I Say"*, *"Great Balls Of Fire"* and *"Good Golly Miss Molly"* he sounds like he has laid the Reeperbahn, St. Pauli and the entire city of Hamburg to waste and combusted himself.

Hank Williams *"Your Cheatin' Heart"* is a romp through the swamps and into Hillbilly heaven where the pace, though not the energy, slows momentarily before the accelerator hits the floor again for *"Hound Dog"*, *"Long Tall Sally"* and a ferocious *"Whole Lotta Shakin' Goin On'"*.

It's a thrill-a-minute record and conjures up a glorious image of Jerry Lee as demonic, deranged, sweat-soaked but vindicated feeding on the applause he'd earned.

46. Adam And The Ants
Kings Of The Wild Frontier (1980)

The original incarnation of Adam And The Ants tried hard to be taken seriously and be respected but the Punk cognoscenti sneered at their silly attempts to seem controversial with their faux decadent interest in fetish, while their delving into dark corners came across as smutty and childish. Still they persevered and a younger crowd of 'Ant People' bought into the band's 'Sex Music' they never swelled in numbers to the point where the Ants would have hits.

A new approach was needed and Malcolm McLaren was hired to act as Svengali to the band, brainstorming sessions about image and sound provided the blueprint of utilising Burundi drumming and adopting a tribal look incorporating Native American trappings. McLaren then dumped the seemingly hapless Adam stealing his Ants for his own ready to launch Burundi powered Bow Wow Wow but before they got to the starting gate Adam had the good fortune to recruit his perfect musical foil, guitarist Marco Pirroni. They quickly wrote an album's worth of songs and put together a two drummer band, one of whom was Chris Hughes a skilled producer, thus the new self-contained Adam and the Ants were ready to go.

The single *"Kings Of The Wild Frontier"* was released in the summer of 1980. I well remember the polarised reactions of their hardcore fan base - many felt betrayed by the band committing the cardinal sin of selling out. The single scraped into the top fifty but in doing so convinced the record company to finance the making of an album. And then they simply exploded into the public consciousness from television screens as *"Dog Eat Dog"* was plucked from the record and became a genuine smash hit.

The album followed suit and Adam And The Ants were pop stars who could do no wrong for two years when it came to scoring hits but found themselves more reviled and ridiculed by critics and their previous supporters than they had ever been before. Not that they worried or had reason to, the album was excellent. It swaggered with confidence and self-assurance, was brim full of hooks, wit and knowing irony underpinned by the tribal drumming and adorned by Marco's guitar flourishes that added a spaghetti western element to the sound which was a glorious miss mash of elements and influences artfully sewn together to create a brand new and very brash and shiny other thing.

"Ant Music" and the re-released title track went swashbuckling up the singles chart accompanied by camp theatrical videos that were discussed in school playgrounds and over work benches nationwide. Elsewhere "Killer In The Home" with its plundered Link Wray riff was atmospheric and brooding and *"Don't Be Square"* and *"The Magnificent Five"* would have made more than adequate singles if they'd been needed to maintain momentum.

The *Prince Charming* album followed and was an even bigger hit although it didn't come close to matching this album's range and dazzling flash. Things went downhill fast for Adam from there with much of his fall gleefully reported in mocking insensitive tabloid headlines that don't do the man any justice and certainly never fail in being completely disrespectful about his musical career which has often been hit and miss but contains this era defining classic.

47. Jellyfish
Bellybutton (1990)

Jellyfish were an anomaly, as the music scene was getting harder and fey guitar bands gave way to the likes of Jane's Addiction and The Pixies, Metal was enjoying one of its periodic upsurges and Hip Hop was accepted by the masses, Jellyfish came along all sunshine, brightly coloured and sweetly harmonic with a sound that harked back to Badfinger, Big Star and Wings in its melodies whilst having the clever rhythmic devices of XTC and the rock crunch of Cheap Trick, they certainly stood out.

This debut album came out to much critical acclaim and fully deserved it. The songs are beautifully crafted and well thought out in the varying approaches spread over the course of the album. The aching lead vocal of singing drummer Andy Sturmer are supported by lush harmonies whilst the bass is nimble, the drums economical, the keyboards bright and occasionally eccentric and Jason Faulkner's guitar playing tasteful and restrained for the most part which adds dramatic impact when he cuts loose with a never gratuitous solo.

Meanwhile the production is as sympathetic and supportive of the material as one would expect from Bee Gees go-to guy Jack Puig who unobtrusively adds layers of strings, muted trumpet and harpsichord into the elegant mix. *"All I Want Is Everything"* and *"The King Is Half Dressed"* along with *"That Is Why"* were promoted via playful savvy videos to which MTV gave heavy rotation. Teen popsters McFly would take a cover version of *"Baby's Coming Back"* to the number one spot in the hit parade many years later proving the commercial potential of the material but all this mattered little as people largely ignored the record.

Edginess was in vogue and the music of Jellyfish, for all its obvious quality, was not edgy. The dysfunctional internal dynamics of the band meant they recorded only one more album, the equally classic and equally poor selling *Spilt Milk*, before calling it a day.

48. Screaming Blue Messiahs

Good And Gone (1984)

THE SCREAMING BLUE MESSIAHS

Feeling pretty dislocated from and disappointment by a lot of the contemporary sounds of the early to mid-Eighties this six-track mini-album came crashing into my orbit revitalising and restoring my mojo and sent shivers running down my spine with its blood-curdling Brutalist and slightly surreal yet back-to-basics brand of raucous Blues tinged Rock & Roll.

Screaming Blue Messiahs were borne out of the break up of Motor Boys Motor, a one Album Beefheart-influenced outfit championed by John Peel.

Drum and bass duties fell to Kenny Harris and Chris Thompson who were masters of tasteful economy, tight as a nut and punchy as hell. Singer guitarist was Bill Carter who didn't so much play the guitar as hammer it until it squealed, splattered in blood from his shredded fingers with which he held up the rhythmic end like a demented cross between Wilko Johnson and Johnny Ramone. His vocal style was equally primal, raging from angry sounding staccato snarls during the quieter passages to demented screams when emphasising a point. They attacked songs and the fact that Harris and Thompson apparently despised Carter further fuelled the tension.

Like Australians The Birthday Party and Americans Gun Club, the Blues were appropriated as a base from which to build but where those two acts were in thrall to the moonshine and rattlesnake sound of the swamps, Screaming Blue Messiahs were informed more by the hard-edged urban blues mixed with elements of Pub and Punk rock.

They were fortunate to hook up with a legendary producer for this record, famed for his work with the likes of Dr Feelgood, Motörhead and Led Zeppelin, he emphasised the muscularity of the band giving them a sound completely at odds with the glitz and glamour of the age. The six tracks were red hot burning coals that slashed like cut throat razors, while Carter sounded like he was sermonising in a fevered insane and close to exhausted state.

It was and remains a thrill-a-minute ride, a compelling masterpiece that in a small way did quite well providing the impetus for three major label albums to follow over the next few years. David Bowie became an über-fan, dropping their name in interviews and inviting them to guest on his *'Glass Spider Tour'* of stadiums and finally forming Tin Machine a kind of Screaming Blue Messiahs tribute act. None of this did them much good; their records didn't sell, they earned no money and remained out of step and unfashionable until the decision to call time on the group became an inevitability.

Time has not seen them grow in stature, nor are they regarded as long-lost treasures, they have not become loved or respected but seem to have been written out of the narrative which is not unexpected but totally undeserved.

49. Al Green
The Belle Album (1977)

In the UK Al Green had a clutch of hit singles although he never troubled the charts with his albums, in the US he was hotter property with all his albums, bar 1967 debut *Back Up Train,* being hits. The release of this album though brought the run to an end, never again would Al Green's records generate sales of any significant quantity. This album in that sense killed his career which strikes me as nuts because not only is it the artistic pinnacle of Al Green's career but is one of those landmark albums to be treasured alongside the likes of Stevie Wonder's *Innervisions,* Marvin Gaye's *What's Going On* and Prince's *1999* – in short it is a stone-cold classic.

1976 was a time of huge change for Al Green; a girlfriend had poured a pan of boiling hot grits over him before killing herself. Al Green would wrestle with the reasons for this tragedy and ultimately turn to the church for solace before eventually being ordained as a minister. Musically there were changes too in a split from producer and mentor Willie Mitchell and the Hi House Band whose signature sound had defined his music for a decade. He assembled a new band, he would self-produce and for the first time he would play guitar on the record where it was elevated high in the mix as lead instrument.

The songs were concerned with God and the search for spiritual salvation over base desires and the album's key line comes in title song "Belle" where the singer states "it's you that I want, but it's him that I need". The songs stretch out meditations on the soul searching that had taken place, they slide on supple grooves which are tastefully delicious. The lyrics are never preachy but more a personal declaration of the next step in the artiste's life. They are joyous affirmations of love and positivity. During *"Chariots Of Fire"* he claims "maybe I can see the possibility of eternity for me". He's optimistic at least and this is carried along on a funk of low end bass and busy drums that give way to the floating sinuous "Dream" where he asks for the happiness of this dream state be allowed to last forever. *The Belle Album* is that rare thing; it is beauty built from the ashes of unhappiness and despair. It is a wondrous thing that was never given much chance at the time of release and still today although the name Al Green is synonymous with all that is good in Soul music, it is regarded as a mere footnote overshadowed by what it followed.

50. The Shadows

The Shadows (1961)

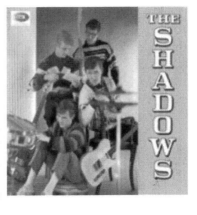

A decade as Cliff Richard's backing band, the fixed rictus grins and Hank Marvin's horn rimmed spectacles, the suits and the Shadows walk, if you set out to assemble the most uncool band of all time and came up with The Shadows, you might think you'd gone too far.

And yet this album, along with Billy Fury's *Sound Of Fury,* is essential British Rock & Roll and the fact that seven of the fourteen tracks were written by various permutations of group members gives the lie to the glib assertion that until The Beatles emerged all British acts were happy to peddle what was served up to them from Tin Pan Alley. The album was begun in 1960 after the phenomenal success of the *"Apache"* single but at that time, in light of the country's economic woes, singles rather than albums were what sold so this collection was recorded during nine separate one day sessions spread over nearly a year on two track equipment with no overdubs.

This was the only Shadows album that featured original members Jet Harris and Tony Meehan on bass and drums and each is given a piece to display their talents on *"Nivram"* and *"See You In My Drums"*. There are also surprisingly three vocal tracks which are none too shoddy as the band tried to avoid being pigeon-holed.

Of course Hank Marvin was the star of the show, he took the guitar as an instrument to places it hadn't been before and his clean playing style had an unhurried elegance underpinned by rhythm guitar extraordinaire provided by the unheralded Bruce Welch.

Rock & Roll was still in its relative infancy and no one could predict its longevity and so the Shadows opted for safety and security playing to the establishment at Royal Variety shows, becoming family entertainers first and foremost and musicians second but this debut album offered a tantalising glimpse of what they could have become if they'd pursued their own youthful agenda.

51. World Of Twist
Quality Street (1991)

World of Twist formed sometime in 1985 in Sheffield with Jamie Fry, the brother of ABC's Martin, on vocals but by the time they'd got organised and begun to realise quite how good they were, there had been a relocation to Manchester and the frontman now was Tony Ogden who had been the drummer.

Once the line-up was settled, they were dizzyingly brilliant. Their shows were happenings full of theatrical flourishes; a mix of high and low tech, a mix of retrospective yearning and dashing futurism and the songs were wonderful. They were tipped for the top - expectations were high. *"The Storm"* was issued as a single and although it was a masterpiece it was not a hit. The even better *"Sons Of The Stage"* followed and sold less, showing a different slower side *"Sweets"* was the third single and was pretty much ignored.

So the record company tried a dance remix of Rolling Stones cover *"She's A Rainbow"*; it rather smacked of desperation and flopped. And so by the time this, the band's only album, was released it was pretty apparent that the moment had passed for World of Twist, they were cursed by being ahead of their time and were already fragmenting. Tony had decided he didn't want to sing anymore, despite the fact that he had matinee idol looks and panache to match his obvious talent in the frontman department.

Quality Street is a superb album, no doubt about it, but it was still a disappointment, anyone who'd ever seen the band knew that the life and magnetism that was in each performance was sorely missing from the record. Still, all their influences were in the mix distilled into the whole that was World of Twist. Conny Plank rubbed shoulders with Joe Meek whose *"This Too Shall Pass Away"* was gloriously interpreted; Northern soul mixed with Acid House, Thunderbirds, Roxy Music, Hawkwind and Stanley Kubrick are all in there too.

It didn't matter because people had moved on and this riot of Pop Art was left behind, unloved by those who, though they'd flirted with it, ultimately had been confused by this kaleidoscope of sound and colour. The tragic deaths of Tony Ogden and Nick Sanderson rekindled tiny pockets of interest in the band but none of it has been sustained and the truth is World of Twist have come to be regarded as no more than a footnote in the 'Madchester' scene of which they were ironically the complete antithesis.

52. Gene Vincent And His Blue Caps

Gene Vincent And His Blue Caps (1957)

Gene Vincent remains an iconic figure in Rock & Roll. People can picture him in black leather snarling into a microphone but though many can reel off the hits enjoyed by the likes of Buddy Holly or Eddie Cochran outside of *"Be-Bop-a Lula"* they simply have no idea about what Gene Vincent And The Blue Caps sounded like, indeed for many the only reason many have heard of him is via Ian Dury And The Blockheads immaculately judged tribute *"Sweet Gene Vincent"*.

So briefly; whilst serving in the US Navy Vincent was involved in a motorcycle accident where insisting his damaged leg not be amputated, the limb was saved but permanently protected by a steel case that caused him agony throughout his life. Discharged from the service he formed Gene Vincent And The Blue Caps featuring early guitar hero Cliff Gallup. He was a passenger in the taxi crash that cost his friend Eddie Cochran his life. A notoriously short-tempered man with a fondness for alcohol, the trigger-happy Vincent shot at Paul Gadd while in Germany during 1968, the future pop star (and convicted paedophile) Gary Glitter fled the country. John Peel released an album by Vincent on his Dandelion Records label. He played his final shows at the *Wooky Hollow* nightclub in Liverpool in 1971 and just a few days later died aged 36 of a ruptured ulcer while visiting his father in California.

In 1974, I made my stage debut at the *Tower Ballroom* in Blackpool. It was a brief, bad-tempered and aggressive performance that perplexed the majority of the audience but one bear-like man in 'Teddy Boy' attire propelled himself towards me and with tears in his eyes promised me that he'd thought Rock & Roll dead until he'd seen me! "Watching you was like seeing Gene Vincent again" he stammered. I was of course elated at this. I loved Gene and knew how honoured I was to receive such a compliment.

On to this record; it was released just four months after its predecessor *Blue Jean Bop*. In the interim, lead guitarist Cliff Gallup and rhythm player Willie Williams had departed from the Blue Caps, although Gallup was brought in to make this album where he truly shines as he cuts loose with a guitar sound that still thrilled when Bryan Gregory borrowed it for The Cramps early records. Gene Vincent coos, squeals and croons in his own inimitable style and the drums and bass are spare and lean. The band are stupendous and keen to show how versatile they are; at one point going from the high energy *"Hold me, Hug me, Rock me"* into a crooned version of *"Unchained Melody"* followed by the country flavoured *"You Told A Fib"* and then a demonic avant-blues howl on *"Catman"*, while the Cliff Gallup penned *"You Better Believe"* with backing vocals from The Jordinaires is magnificent.

Although it is from an era when albums were heavily padded with filler, this record is 100% killer. A real team effort from a band with that magical ability of each player supporting and complementing the others creating a confident sure-footed whole. Unfortunately this would be the last time Gene and his original Blue Caps would get to make an album together but what a satisfying record they left behind.

53. The Cannonball Adderley Quintet
Accent On Africa (1968)

Miles Davis had released *Sketches Of Spain* as far back as 1959. It was highly popular and quite rightly received high acclaim for its impressionistic imaginings of rich culture filtered through the prism of American Jazz.

In 1968, in cahoots with producer David Axelrod in his most inventive period and with genius arranger HB Barnum, famed for his work with artists as diverse as Count Basie and Frank Sinatra to The Supremes and Aretha in tow, Cannonball Adderley cut this precursor to 'World Music' in similarly impressionistic style. It is a genius record but was ignored and forgotten almost as soon as it was released.

Though billed as being by the quintet, the music is clearly played by a big band so as well as the credited Julian Adderley and drummer Earl Palmer the probability is that Joe Zawinul played keyboards as he composed one track and others contributed further guitar and bass parts alongside a bevy of percussionists who give the record a chunky, funky vibe. *"Ndo Lima"* opens the record in spooky exotic style with a drone played on cornet. Congas and other percussion come into the mix before the horns and a heavenly chorus of female vocals signify the coming of light. *"Hamba Nami"* follows and is a playful, strutting warm-hearted piece. Wes Montgomery's *"Up and At It"* is a feast of uplifting screeching saxes and vocal chants while *"Gun-Jah"* referencing a Marijuana-like intoxicant, is an ambient piece that explodes in its final moment. *"Lemadima"* finishes the record in galloping style.

The record in its entirety sounds like a film soundtrack; orchestral in scope and depth. Peppered by snippets of African vocal harmonies, the groove of a Southern Baptist church and cascading through it the Dinner Jazz formality of the big band create a highly unique and at times seemingly contradictory sound.

I don't know why a record this good wasn't lauded half a century ago when it was released, I don't know why since then it's not been picked up on and proclaimed as the lost classic that it truly is, what I do know is music this sensuous and soulful makes life that much richer for those who embrace it.

54. Bob Marley and The Wailers
Natty Dread (1974)

What is Bob Marley doing in here you may ask? Cultural icon, the first Third World superstar, loved and respected all over the globe, yes – all true! But hip? No, most definitely not. Even in his lifetime there existed that inverted snobbery that pushed the view that his music was 'Reggae-lite', an inauthentic sell-out to the money men of Babylon.

The likes of Dennis Brown and Gregory Isaacs were regarded as superior artists and more deserving of success which is utter balderdash! As fine as those two artists are, Marley was streets ahead in terms of creativity and his desire to engage in matters of importance. In death Bob has become legend, an image (he is as much a poster as the Ramones are a T-Shirt) and the presence of his greatest hits album is obligatory in most CD collections, yet his run of superb albums released throughout the Seventies are considered inessential, as they are too much trouble to listen to.

Natty Dread was his first album without fellow Wailers Bunny and Peter Tosh. It his first under his own name and the first that utilised vocal trio, the I Threes. *"Lively Up Yourself"* is a sparkling uplifting opening track similar in sentiment to "Get Up Stand Up" but less declaratory. *"No Woman No Cry"* slipped into fond reminiscences of the powerful influence of old friends in hard times. *"Them Belly Full (But We Hungry)"* cautions that, 'a hungry man is an angry man' and *"Rebel Music (3 O'Clock Roadblock)"* speaks of the frightening reality of being stopped at army checkpoints, it is indignant and defiant. Marley was coming up with the goods in terms of supplying brilliant material on this pivotal album but of note too was the excellence of the production which gives the record an intimate warm feel. The contributions from the I Threes enhances the soulfulness of the record while the musicians are absolutely faultless, the drums and bass propel the songs inventively, the often bluesy lead guitar embellishes them and the horns add texture and punctuation. Nothing is overplayed, each note counts, it is exquisite.

"So Jah Say" and *"Natty Dread"* are songs of faith. While the deliciously seductive *"Bend Down Low"* is most definitely an ode to more earthly delights while *"Talkin' Blues"* and *"Revolution"* return to political comment.

Probably the best album of Marley's career, it expresses much of what concerned the man, from the spiritual to the carnal with a healthy dose of the reality of Kingston's streets thrown in for good measure, it shouldn't be neglected.

55. Elvis Presley

Elvis Is Back! (1960)

We all think we know the narrative arc of the career of Elvis Aaron Presley; in the accepted biography he goes from cutting revolutionary Rock & Roll sides for Sam Phillips at Sun Records, before transferring to RCA where his first two albums, containing the likes of "Heartbreak Hotel" and "Hound Dog", make him a worldwide sensation - the undisputed 'King of Rock & Roll'. He is then called up into the army and returns neutered and makes a series of terrible films before regaining control of his career with the recording of the masterful Memphis Sessions before succumbing to the evil intentions of Colonel Tom Parker who sells him body and soul to the showbiz hell of Las Vegas where he falls prey to a combination of prescription drugs and hamburgers and dies slumped on a Graceland toilet in 1977.

It is a neat and tidy parable of American Rock culture. So it is little wonder then that his post-army output is regarded as kitsch and incredibly unhip when that is not even remotely the case. To the very end Elvis was capable of making fabulous records, his last album contained both *"Burnin Love"* and *"Way Down"*, both excellent while this, his first post-army album, might well be the best collection of his career outside of greatest hits compilations, displaying a versatility and confidence coupled with the sheer joy of being back doing what he loved best after an enforced absence.

Recorded in two sessions during March and April 1960 and using much of his original Sun Records band including Scotty Moore, Floyd Cramer and D.J Fontana with The Jordanaires featured heavily on Doo-Wop flavoured backing vocals and Elvis himself playing rhythm guitar, the album switches effortlessly between styles without stepping out of character and creating a prototype that The Beatles, for one, would imitate a few years later.

Elvis, whose voice was remarkable anyway, had also been working on it during his army stint; improving his breath control and somehow adding a full octave to his vocal range, he never sounded better. There isn't a poor song on this record and it's hard to pick stand-outs but some glorious moments are "Fever" a recent hit for Peggy Lee which Elvis slinks his way through over a finger clicking beat, *"Dirty Dirty Feeling"* is a twinkle in the eye playful romp while Lowell Fulson's Blues classic *"Baby Reconsider"* is a gritty low moan that balances moments of near operatic splendour while *"Such a Night"* and *"Soldier Boy"* are worthy of high praise as well.

Elvis is Back was a superb album and when you consider that during the two days recording *"Stuck On You"*, *"Are You Lonesome Tonight?"*, *"It's Now Or Never"*, *"A Mess Of Blues"* and other tracks were also recorded for standalone singles, it is clear what a streak of creative enthusiasm Elvis was enjoying, he was a force of nature – Elvis was King!

56. The Who
Tommy (1969)

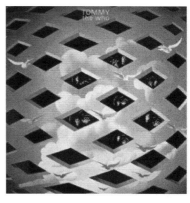

Hugely acclaimed on release for its daring inventiveness, the phrase 'Rock Opera' added gravitas to *Tommy* meaning the audience could slap their own backs and be self-satisfied for understanding such clever conceptual music.

Was it the first 'Rock Opera'? Or had The Pretty Things with *SF Sorrow* or The Kinks with *Village Green Preservation Society* beaten The Who to the punch? *Tommy* was wrapped in a bubble of self-importance. The subsequent stage musicals and film only magnified this, yet gradually the tide of popular opinion turned. The Who came to be seen as essentially a blunt instrument bludgeoning their way through ever more pretentious and hypocritical material. The were critically reassessed and judged as inferior to contemporaries over whom they had once towered. Then came Pete Townshend's public tainting over downloaded child sex images; his explanation, while wholly consistent with his questing nature may have been accepted by the authorities but mud sticks and his and The Who's reputation suffered further and *Tommy* in particular was targeted as being overblown, grandiose and not very good; the wheel had turned full circle.

Yet *Tommy* is a great album. It is among the best albums of the Sixties, and is easily The Who's best work. It is beautifully played and written and though the plot is convoluted, it doesn't matter. Enjoy the quality of the songs, the story is only a device to stimulate the writing process and is not of huge importance.

The Who never played more softly or with such subtlety, there is no grandstanding or macho posturing. They sing and play as an ego-free unit. Nothing superfluous is allowed, every note supports the song. And what songs! Townshend writes superbly, completely engaged in expressing his spiritual journey having become a follower of 'avatar' Meher Baba whose values of compassion, love and introspection struck a chord with the conflicted guitarist. He was ably abetted by John Entwistle, whose musicality often knits pieces together and whose prowess as a brass player adds immeasurably to the sound, while his black humour on his brace of songs is perfectly judged in the context of the album. Roger Daltrey sings wonderfully, his phrasing immaculate, while Keith Moon is in his element and not tied to laying down a steady beat but 'playing the song' and adding embellishments where he sees fit.

Considering that this album contains *"Amazing Journey"* a brilliant interpretation of Sonny Boy Williamson's *"Eyesight For The Blind"; "The Acid Queen",* Entwistle's *"Cousin Kevin"* and *"Fiddle About"*, *"Pinball Wizard"* (condemned as 'distasteful ' by Radio One's Tony Blackburn), *"Sensation"*, *"Sally Simpson"* written after a gig with The Doors descended into violence, *"I'm Free"* and finally, *"We're Not Gonna Take It"* then anyone who seriously suggests that this is anything but a record to be cherished and a monumental achievement either has incredibly poor taste or is stone deaf!

57. Montrose
Montrose (1973)

Heavy Metal is generally derided by hipsters as they dig through the record crates of musical culture, yet it still cannot be completely dismissed by them and so records by Black Sabbath, Led Zeppelin, Motörhead, Guns n' Roses, Metallica and even the likes of Def Leppard and Iron Maiden are permissible to name check while strangely this most heavy and even more metal platter is for the most part ignored.

Montrose was put together and named after Ronnie Montrose following his departure from the Edgar Winter Band hot on the heels of the success of their *They Only Come Out At Night* album containing the immense hit *"Frankenstein"*. Long considered heir apparent to Jimmy Page, Montrose recruited Bill Church on bass who he'd played alongside on Van Morrison sessions and Unknown's drummer Denny Carmassi and vocalist Sammy Hagar. He and Hagar pretty much split the writing and they set about introducing themselves in uncompromising style. In an era where there was a general mellowing of sound among the hard rock fraternity, epitomised by the chart successes of Boston and Bachman Turner Overdrive, these boys blasted out jagged slabs of noise.

Concrete thick riffs predominated and Hagar delivered dumb, honest, bratty lyrics as if he was racing the clock to have his say. Of the first three tracks on this album; *"Rock the Nation"*, *"Bad Motor Scooter"* and *"Space Station #5"*, the first two were must have singles of the day; short and sharp and full of Punk Rock energy and attitude, almost like The MC5 but without the white panther manifesto. The latter is a blazing monster of a thing shooting off on tangents with a titanic main riff filched a few years down the line by Stiff Little Fingers for their *"Suspect Device"* single. *"I Don't Want It"* finishes side one in fine declaratory style and side two opens again echoing The MC5 in *"Back in the USA"* mode by taking a Rock & Roll classic and running a jolting stomach-churning charge through it – Roy Brown's *"Good Rockin' Tonight"* is the innocent victim of the assault. *"Rock Candy"* takes the Led Zeppelin route of a grinding riff played over titanic sounding drums whilst Hagar heroically tries to imbue the simplistic lyrics with emotion before *"One Thing On My Mind"* swaggers but doesn't quite satisfy but the album closes with another devilish riff played over thundering drums on *"Make It Last"* making this debut album a very satisfactory feast for anyone who has ever loved the sound of a band holding nothing back.

Sadly, Church left shortly after quickly followed by Hagar as Ronnie Montrose decreed they lose their Brutalist crunch and jagged edges for a smoother more commercial but sonically lacklustre future.

58. The Kinks
Muswell Hillbillies (1971)

"You keep all your smart modern writers, give me William Shakespeare,

You keep your smart modern painters, I'll take Rembrandt, Da Vinci, Titian and Gainsborough"

Track one side one and the great classicist Raymond Douglas Davies nails his colours to the mast in appreciation of works of substance over the ephemeral and... hip.

In terms of quality and strength of songs, The Kinks were the equal of The Beatles in the Sixties, although they were never indulged with the same lavish production on their records or extensive studio time to allow experimentation. The Kinks were more a shoestring operation and yet they consistently came up with music of real substance and for that they are loved by anyone with even a modicum of discernment. Loved that is for their Sixties records, the run of glorious hits and albums like *Face to Face* and *Village Green Preservation Society* through to the Seventies up until *Lola vs the Powermen*. The orthodox opinion is that after changing labels they started making dull concept albums as Ray Davies lost his gift for concise and melodic music that became verbose and tuneless. There is some merit in that opinion, harsh though it may seem, but only if *Muswell Hillbillies* is ignored which it pretty much has been since the day it was released selling a fraction of the amount of their previous album and failing to make even the lowest positions of the charts. It is the unloved runt in the Kinks litter where even the derided concept albums are remembered and occasionally dusted off to be revisited yet *Muswell Hillbillies*, the record I love more than any other in this book, is simply airbrushed from history.

The record is very loosely conceptual, concerning itself with the beginning of gentrification and social displacement and is full of vignettes concerned with the problems faced by members of the community; the dreamers, the misfits and the mentally ill. It is a beautifully compassionate big-hearted record that is impossible to not be moved by. For the first time the brass section of The Mike Cotton Sound was added and only the opening track *"20th Century Man"*, a madly schizophrenic and angry tune, could be classified as a rocker while elsewhere the Nashville via North London country stylings lend the album a curious old time quality, the reason perhaps that it alienated their audience. Perhaps, in an era of flash super-groups The Kinks seemed antiquated and tame? Perhaps people should have tried a little harder and listened but they didn't and missed the deliciously wobbling *"Acute Schizophrenia Paranoia Blues"*, the sorry saga evoked in *"Alcohol"* and the joy of a chorus proclaiming "Life is overrated, Life is complicated, I've gotta get away from this complicated life" and the optimism that everything can be fixed if we *"Have A Cup Of Tea"* before the tear-jerking *"Oklahoma USA"* which sees the protagonist disappearing into a fog of romantic illusion rather than confront the numbing reality of being trapped.

The characters portrayed are superbly observed, their sad lives laid out before us with empathy and sadness. If Charles Dickens had utilised the medium of music "Great Expectations" would no doubt have sounded much like this hidden masterpiece.

59. Frankie Goes To Hollywood

Welcome To The Pleasuredome (1984)

Oversized 'Frankie Says' T-Shirts were *de rigueur* on every high street in the country during the mid 1980s, as the Liverpool band took their subversive messages into the very heart of the mainstream. Gay sex was presented as a celebratory revolutionary act, and as the world seemed to be teetering on the brink of nuclear oblivion, Frankie ridiculed US president Ronald Reagan and USSR supremo Leonid Brezhnev for their crass stupidity delivering a clear anti-authoritarian message.

Puritans were horrified and straight society recoiled while Frankie continued in turn to tease and sneer at reactionary thought and deed. Frankie were a high-art finger on the pulse phenomenon who reached from the gutter towards the stars and made records that were statements and made their statements events. These were underdogs having their day and relishing the opportunity to inflict on the world brash, opinionated, challenging and provocative dance-friendly floor-filling delights of glittering excess... and then it stopped. The T-Shirts filled charity shops, the records following them in short order as Frankie didn't fade away but simply disappeared to be erased from the national consciousness as quickly as they'd arrived. Even on a local level if talk turns to a post Beatles Liverpool music scene the likes of Echo and the Bunnymen, Wah Heat, Shack and The Boo Radleys are likelier to be reminisced over than the Frankies. Even Big in Japan and The Spitfire Boys, where Holly Johnson and Paul Rutherford cut their respective teeth, elicit a warmer response.

A cackling voice declares "the world is our oyster" to open

the homo-erotically sleeved artefact that is Welcome to the Pleasuredome, famously produced and conceived by studio master and conceptualist Trevor Horn who for the recording process dispensed with the band in favour of more polished musicians. Let not that become a licking stick for this album though because the ends indisputably justified the means. The enormous hits are of course contained in remixed forms and remain absolutely thrilling to these ears; "Relax" rides on that sinuous bassline and the surge towards its climax is sheer bliss, *"Two Tribes"* is powerful in its blatant condemnation of the superpowers and re-emphasised by the cover of Edwin Starr's Motown classic *"War"* while *"The Power Of Love"* is a beautiful piece of music that is double-edged and cutting in its obvious insincerity, while *"Krisco Kisses"* is a funky gem and a wild romp through *"Born to Run"* emphasise that it's not just the singles that carry a punch, the whole record is a gleaming galloping symphony of over-the-top studio sounds and statements that were and remain a glorious triumph.

60. Sinéad O'Connor
I Do Not Want What I Haven't Got [

On the back of the monumental success of *"Nothing Compares 2 U"*, the obscure Prince song reinvented as a requiem for her mother who had died in a car crash five years earlier, this album became a huge seller and seemed to herald the coming of a big star. However Sinéad O'Connor's emotional intensity proved to be far too frightening a prospect for that to happen and despite being blessed with wonderful talent and a singularity of purpose, in speaking her truth and exposing hypocrisy she has become reviled rather than revered. Marginalised and dismissed as a crackpot for her refusal to fit into acceptable and easily bracketed roles, she presented the music industry with a strong opinionated woman when they wanted a weak needy girl.

She opens this, her second album, with *"Feel So Different"* which begins with "the serenity prayer" written by Reinhold Niebuhr and follows that with *"I Am Stretched On Your Grave"*, an anonymous Seventeenth-century Irish poem set to music and incorporating James Brown's *"Funky Drummer"* in its rhythm. Both are striking and uncompromising, the music covers much ground on the album moving from folk to up-tempo rock as on the Marco Pirroni (of Adam and the Ants fame) co-written "Jump In The River" while deploying a near Trip-Hop feel on *"Nothing Compares 2 U"*.

Lyrically there is much soul baring and examining of situations and feelings arising from them, her recent split from the father of her first-born is addressed throughout; "two years ago the seed was planted but since then you have taken me for granted" she sings in the emotionally charged *"The Last Day Of Our Acquaintance"*. Elsewhere on the acoustic *"Black Boys On Mopeds"* she prophetically sings "these are dangerous days, to say what you mean is to dig your own grave" there are digs at Margaret Thatcher and England before the album closes with the title track, a six minute a cappella hymn for redemption.

61. Elvis Costello and The Attractions
Blood and Chocolate (1986)

Coming riding on a white charger over the hill in 1977, Elvis made confessional singer-songwriting hip again as part of Stiff Records roster of seemingly lovable ultra-talented misfits but behind the witty advertising strategies of his label and the horn rimmed spectacles lurked an extremely prickly character who made plenty of enemies.

While he was on a roll and his records remained of the highest quality he was untouchable, but he started into the Eighties with *Goodbye Cruel World* and then *Punch The Clock,* both tired sounding records lacking any spark of originality that were sterile and soulless. Those who had been waiting in the wings for such a slip were quick to pounce, knives out and pencils sharpened Costello came under attack. His perceived arrogance, his rudeness and his too-clever-by-half persona had built up resentment, now it was safe to attack him.

Once his audience began to dwindle he was stripped of armour and even his appearance was scorned. No doubt the personal nature of much of the criticism was wounding but the attacks on his music were to a large degree justifiable. He set about addressing that with his early 1986 *King of America* album, a spare rootsy record helmed by T-Bone Burnett and featuring a bevy of red hot musicians in place of The Attractions. It was a smart move and undeniably a very good piece of work but what to do for a follow up? We didn't need to wait too long to find out as just months later came *Blood and Chocolate*.

An angry, ugly screech of guitar announces opening track *"Uncomplicated"* before drums that sound like a skull being pummelled by a piece of lead pipe and a wild organ crash-in with Costello barking in hostile accusatory fashion over the repeated two-chord maelstrom. The Attractions were back in place and early producer Nick Lowe returned to chair proceedings. The sound was similar to the first album The Attractions featured on, 1978's *This Year's Model* but almost a decade on the players sound tougher and harder, a more imposing proposition.

To try and get the album done without animosities derailing the process, the band were recorded playing songs they didn't know. A couple of takes was the only luxury allowed and it makes for a thrillingly brutal record. Lyrically and vocally this was Costello at his peak coming off the back of a painful divorce, the songs bristle with barely concealed anger. They're spiteful and sarcastic and where we had heard Costello introspectively examining his hurt and despair, this time the songs were outward vengeful attacks. On the vicious *"Hope You're Happy Now"* he delivers line after line of scornful derision, "I knew then what I know now, I never loved you anyhow, I hope you're happy now…" and in the deceptively tender sounding *"Home is Anywhere You Lay Your Head"* the delicious couplet, "…he's contemplating murder - he must be in love…" is casually dropped.

Everywhere there is deceit and despair; cuckolds, drunks and emotions bordering on the psychotic. There is "Tokyo Storm Warning" which resembles Bob Dylan as he slaloms downhill through some psychedelic shopping mall where they sell *"Japanese God Toys"* and we have *"Battered Old Bird"* full of sad bitterness, *"Next Time Around"* which is disguised as being jaunty and optimistic but as you listen to the words coming from Costello's mouth you realise hate is the emotion being expressed. There is also "I Want You" which is one of the most staggeringly brilliant performances ever committed to wax. A six minute crawl through the emotional debris contained inside the dangerously sick soul of the obsessed, rejected lover who can't let go, "I want to know he knows you now after only guessing, it's the thought of him undressing you, or you undressing, I WANT YOU!" It is an uncomfortable listen but so insightful at the same time, it is the truly electrifying high point of this superb album that forced the words back down the critics' throats, although it became the worst selling record of Costello's career at that point as he was yesterday's news in the eye of the general public.

62. Elton John

Goodbye Yellow Brick Road (1973)

A very long time ago, before he become an agony aunt for pop stars with drug problems, a pantomime dame, a practised chat show fixture, a clothes horse, a knight and friend of the royals, a football club owner and tabloid fodder, Elton John used to be a musician and a very good one at that, blessed with a wonderful gift for being able to write gorgeously memorable songs around the often bizarre lyrics provided by Bernie Taupin and to deliver them soulfully and expressively in a warm rich voice that seemed to flow like honey.

This was the last album he made as a musician rather than a celebrity. This double platter was so stuffed with hits that Elton's hard won success became stratospheric and was closely followed by megalomania, complacency and the draining away of his talent as fame for fame's sake took a tight grip.

Like a lot of Elton's best albums this is a schizophrenic set of the serious, the salacious and the silly but contains brilliant rockers that endeared him to his audience. The dirge-like near prog *"Funeral For A Friend"* crawls through the opening eleven minutes of the record which was a bold move but is followed by the peon to both dead Hollywood icon Marilyn Monroe and childhood innocence *"Candle In The Wind"* - so far so maudlin, but the gloriously silly funky falsetto of *"Benny And The Jets"* follows and from there we are treated to three sides of diverse high quality material such *"Sweet Painted Lady"* about prostitution and the lesbian ode *"All The Girls Love Alice"*. There is the epic *"Grey Seal"*, a return to the country rock he'd utilised on 1970's *Tumbleweed Connection* with *"Social Disease"* before a tribute to another icon on the warm-hearted *"Roy Rogers"* and piano bashing stompers in *"Your Sister Can't Twist (But She Can Rock & Roll)"* and *"Saturday Night's Alright For Fighting"* before the majestic final track *"Harmony"* brings to a close an album where the depth of talent, inventiveness and vitality of its creator are fully displayed.

63. Gilbert O'Sullivan
Himself (1971)

"What is this?" we asked when Gilbert O'Sullivan appeared for the first time on our television screens dressed in an outfit that looked like a cross between a Depression Era urchin and a Hovis advert. In his own way O'Sullivan was de-constructing the accepted way in which musicians presented themselves, much as the Sex Pistols did five years later. It was certainly a striking though unflattering image and one initiated by the artist himself against management wishes. As strangely fascinating as the singer looked, easily the most amazing part of the performance was the song he sang *"Nothing Rhymed"* which was devastating in its weaving of imagery and Spike Milligan-like playful subversion of everyday phrases, it was at once surreal and poignant. On the evidence of just one song there was no doubting that this strange-looking man was a huge unique talent.

Himself arrived later that year after the excellent flop single *"Underneath The Blanket Go"*, wrapped in a sleeve of sepia-tinted images mimicking an old photograph album. It is a masterful record; evocative, tuneful and full of pertinent well-thought-out lyrics recalling Randy Newman on his finest form and displaying the percussive piano style O'Sullivan had accidentally developed when transitioning from drums to keyboard.

There is a short introduction to the record and then the first track proper *"January Git"* comes in on a swinging old style horn arrangement and a bright as a button cheerful vocal "...full of razzmatazz...", *"Bye-Bye"* manages to be a song about parting that escapes the clichéd maudlin quality of so many songs dealing with the same topic. *"Permissive Twit"* is a brilliant song about the pain of an unwanted pregnancy, O'Sullivan displaying his knack for capturing the drama in ordinary lives. *"Matrimony"* is another single, a humorous take on the institution of marriage before side one closes with *"Nothing Rhymed"*. Side two maintains the high quality from start to finish *"Too Much Attention"* is a critique of negative thinkers from the perspective of the negative thinker incorporating a riff of hard hit piano and flute, the up-tempo *"Thunder and Lightning"* gives way to the ambitious *"Houdini Said"* containing a lyric of bewilderment at the destructive tendencies of the privileged over an imaginative cinematic backing before the album concludes with the upbeat *"Doing the Best I Can"* and a short outro segment signalling the end of a superlative debut album. There were still artistic triumphs to come such as the wonderful *"Alone Again Naturally"*, but within a few years artistic redundancy and a Kevin Keegan perm were what came to mind when considering Gilbert O.

64. The Saints
Prehistoric Sounds
(1978)

Scruffy and greasy looking, with a genuine air of aggression about them, these guys were never likely to want to join or be invited to join the fraternity of British Punk Rockers they found awaiting them when they relocated from their native Australia in 1977. They stood apart, disdaining the dumb fashion victims of the scene because they were the real thing in a sea of fakes. They were too sharp and intelligent to allow anybody to misrepresent them, they were deadly serious about what they were doing, not opportunists having a good time looking to score a quick buck. They were The Saints one of the greatest and least compromised groups in the history of Rock & Roll.

Their *"I'm Sstranded"* single pre-dated all their British equivalents' releases and its snarling feral glory savaged the competition. Up against The Saints bands like The Clash and Sex Pistols sounded limp, effete and lacking authenticity.

Now, two years down the line, came their third and, in their original incarnation, final album. The first had been a high energy guitar-led classic, the second saw Stax-like horns added to the mix and was even better. This new one was more ambitious, utilising brass instrumentation as the bedrock of the sound rather than mere punctuation; it was audacious and saw much of the small fan-base they'd amassed turn their back on them once and for all, leaving the album to languish unloved in record shop racks and persuading the record company that this surly bunch had no commercial potential and were no longer worth investing in. That The Saints were unpopular and *Prehistoric Sounds* was completely out of step with fashion are two undeniable facts, a third fact though is it was a record of sheer genius.

The album was made in conflict, the principal writers Chris Bailey and Ed Kuepper were pulling in completely different directions as singer Bailey wanted to follow a straight-ahead mix of pop/rock songs while guitarist Kuepper favoured a much more left-field approach which he would go on to pursue with The Laughing Clowns. Whether the tensions and air of unpleasantness caused by the disagreements bled into the performances is difficult to discern but the intensity is high throughout the thirteen tracks even if the tempos have dropped, the power remains and is harnessed in a bravura display of controlled sneering as showcased in the outstanding *"Brisbane (Security City)"* where Bailey pours out a tale of disdain and resentment at the oppression the band encountered at the hand of the law in their earliest days over a dragging cyclical riff before it gives way to a furious thrilling explosion. *"Swing For Crime"* and *"All Times Through Paradise"* come close to matching this, while *"Everyday's a Holiday, Every Night's a Party"* drips with unveiled sarcasm and a run through of Otis Redding's *"Security"* and Aretha's *"Save Me"* take them close to the sound of Van Morrison in his garage punk splendour when fronting Them.

65. Nic Jones

Penguin Eggs (1980)

Inside the often precious world inhabited by folk music aficionados, Nic Jones and his music are much loved and highly revered but somehow his reputation has never gained a wider audience in the way that the work of Bert Jansch and Shirley Collins has.

For rockers, punks, jazz enthusiasts and ravers theirs are names that can be casually inserted into a conversation to illustrate what a sweeping breadth of taste one has and how open-minded one is, while Nic Jones remains much more marginal, probably due to the horrific road accident he was involved in driving home from a gig at Glossop Folk Club. After falling asleep at the wheel, Jones crashed into a wagon smashing his body to pieces. Emerging from a coma to find his whole right side needed reassembling and parts replacing he said "I'm an illusion. The only thing not bust was my guitar." The accident effectively ended his career, leaving the few albums he'd recorded to do his talking,

The last of those, *Penguin Eggs,* is his masterpiece. Purely acoustic, his open-tuned guitar style is delightfully engaging and always interesting, his laconic vocal delivery untainted by artifice. Sparing use of recorder and melodeon and harmony vocals add all the flesh that is required to this rich and bright delight of an album. Each song tells a story in the English folk tradition that is magical and engaging, for these are not dusty and impenetrable dirges aimed at a closeted few but superbly arranged songs full of life made relevant for the modern age. Never one to suffer fools or be constrained by conventions, Nic Jones refreshed the whole folk genre with this bold and classy album.

66. Them

The Angry Young Them

(1965)

While lacking in the thematic flow of his later solo work, this debut album cut by Them is the best place to look for evidence of the sparks that ignite the soul of Van Morrison, here there is not merely an undercurrent of 'attitude' but in your face irrefutable menace delivered belligerently without compromise. As the band play prowling, lean, spiky R&B in their signature style honed during their legendary nights at Belfast's Maritime Hotel, Them was clearly a dynamic proposition armed with Morrison's burgeoning song-writing prowess who should have flourished in their own right but instead were somewhat overshadowed by the huge popularity of the similar sounding Rolling Stones. Retrospective interest has been scant as Morrison, resentful of the business dealings that cheated and poisoned the band, pretty much eliminated the period from his past.

Six of the tracks are Morrison originals alongside a clutch written by manager Bert Berns and covers of the likes of John Lee Hooker and Jimmy Reed. Kicking off with the immortal *"Mystic Eyes"* recorded and edited down from a long spontaneous jam, this is an audacious piece far ahead of its time that tears up conventional structure. A defiantly Irish accented Morrison opens up track *two* *"If You and I Could Be as Two"* in a spoken word preamble to a snaking blues, *"Little Girl"* finds the unhinged sounding Morrison screaming "...I've got you in my soul" over spooked organ trills. *"Just a Little Bit"* utilises horns, another unusual move for 1965 rockers, which emphasises that Them were leaders.

"Gloria" of course is unquestionably one of the cornerstones of contemporary music, it is sheer perfection from its intoxicating

main riff, its thrilling call and response chorus, its breakdown to a snail-paced vehicle for Morrison's wild vocals and recurring guitar figure, it is the aural equivalent of a Picasso. *"You Just Can't Win"* is another Morrison original that marks him as a special talent as he weaves a tale and takes us journeying through specific locations with him. John Lee Hooker's *"Don't Look Back"* becomes a delicate soulful ballad. *"I Like It Like That"* is a statement of strutting defiance, "...don't call me, I'll call you..." sneers Van. *"I'm Gonna Dress in Black"* which sound-wise echoes the treatment The Animals gave *"House of the Rising Sun"* is a song perfectly tailored for Them to stretch out on, it fits like a glove. *"Bright Lights Big City"* and *"Route 66"* are sprightly run-throughs of the standards that peppered the band's live sets. And there we have it, a rather unheralded mini masterpiece as an opening salvo from one of the iconic figures of contemporary music hiding in plain sight and worthy of much respect and love.

67. Dory Previn
Mythical Kings and Iguanas (1971)

From the late Fifties through the Sixties, Dory Previn was a successful lyricist for Hollywood film scores, her songs tackled by Frank Sinatra, Marilyn Monroe, Bobby Darin and Dionne Warwick who took Previn's *"Theme From the Valley of the Dolls"*. However, her idyllic life was shattered when she discovered her husband André Previn was conducting an affair with young actress Mia Farrow who had become pregnant by him, as the marriage collapsed her sense of betrayal led to a breakdown.

She was hospitalised and received electro-convulsive shock therapy. This was the backdrop to the records she began to release beginning with *On The Way to Where* in 1970 which was introspective and confessional to an almost forensic degree. A year later came this record, *Mythical Kings and Iguanas*, it finds Previn examining life in a deeply personal, unflinching manner. Her words are scalpel-sharp and honest yet retain a beautiful poetic rhythm over a baroque folk backing that's jazz tinged and although there are an orchestra of musicians and backing singers utilised, the sound is never cluttered or in danger of swamping the singer or her songs.

"Angels and Devils the Following Day" is a track where Previn's insight into relationships is displayed vividly as she compares two lovers, one rough who may cause physical bruising, the other gentle on the surface but who tortures psychologically, *"Lemon Haired Ladies"* and *"The Lady With The Braid"* are concerned with insecurity and human frailties delivered in the deadpan manner of someone desperately trying to hold themselves together. *"Stone for Bessie Smith"* has appropriate blues styling and laments the sad passing of the troubled Janis Joplin with empathy and sensitivity. *"The Game"* is a troubled reflection on life and love that shifts shape whilst never losing it's cynicism that "...the game is fixed..." and then finally the acceptance that there's no changing it "...deal me in..." she concludes.

This is such a good record, full of great songs of wisdom and intelligence, the low monotone of the singer supported by a gospel chorus on the title track and its reprise that closes the album is heavily reminiscent of Leonard Cohen, another poetic soul possessed of great humanity.

68. The Fatima Mansions

Viva Dead Ponies (1991)

This album was originally to be entitled *Bugs Fucking Bunny* and that it was changed to the more palatable and tasteful *Viva Dead Ponies* can only have been for artistic reasons because Fatima Mansions did not countenance compromise, be it causing a near riot while supporting U2 in Milan by insulting the Pope and football or in the nature of the albums they made containing fiercely intelligent songs that never tiptoed around a subject.

The Fatima Mansions were formed by Cathal Coughlan following the demise of Microdisney and this, their second album, finds them leaving behind the soft synth style of the previous album and band for a chunkier guitar led approach.

These were a dynamic bunch who could go from the gentle to the explosive in the blink of an eye while Cathal Coughlan flicked between a Scott Walker like croon to a Gibby Haynes type of screeching howl. They pack each facet of their style into opening track *"Angel's Delight"* where, over a bed of bubbling synth, we hear the singer coo, "…kill a cop – why the hell not…" before abruptly the track lurches into industrial hard rock territory, backwards and forwards it goes so you're never allowed to slip into a comfort zone. Throughout the album there are brief interludes, snippets of tunes that just as they begin to take shape give way to the next track proper. If this sounds a little too self conscious and pretentious fear not, for within the experimentation is a beating pop heart and we are treated to glorious melodies and hooks that could quite feasibly yielded genuine subversive chart hits, *"Thursday"* certainly bears that out, though elsewhere epics like *"White Knuckle Express"* with its "...halls full of corpses..." would certainly have proved a little too challenging even with the epic James Bond-style. Equally hard-hitting is the very much to the point *"Chemical Cosh"*. Title track *"Viva Dead Ponies"* utilises disturbing imagery over a perverse power ballad track that twists as it swells and is quite breathtaking.

Though The Fatima Mansions are all but forgotten these days, a listen to their music is as invigorating and inspiring as it ever was.

69. Stackridge

Stackridge (1971)

Charming is the word that springs to mind when I think of Stackridge. They were hopelessly out of step with the times when they released this stunning debut and never caught up. They channelled elements of Frank Zappa, Max Wall, Peter Paul and Mary, Kevin Ayers and Enid Blyton into a gently rib-tickling brew with eccentric instrumentation and precisely mannered English vocals; for two and a half albums they were, to me at least, irresistibly lovely – a semi-secret treasure.

The album begins with the Beatlesque *"Grande Piano"* that if dropped into *The White Album* would go unnoticed before the folk jig of *"Dora the Female Explorer"* takes us in another direction, it's like Lindisfarne on a diet of Scrumpy and acid rather than brown ale and dope. There were plans afoot for the characters portrayed in the songs to appear in cartoon book form aimed at the children's market, sadly that idea never took wing. *"Percy the Penguin"* (who has cucumber wings) is a brassy fantasy similar to the things John Lennon wrote in his Lear influenced stage.

A wide soundscape, orchestral in its scope, closes side one in *"Essence of Porphyry"* displaying a prog style similar to that of early

Genesis. "*Marigold Conjunction*" is a swinging (West) Country track and "*West Mall*" references a shared flat in Clifton, Bristol.

The album closer "*Slark*" is a fourteen-minute epic at turns quaint and sinister as the tale of an innocent motorist driving in his "creosote car" sees from the darkening sky the monster Slark appear. Appeals for mercy are ignored as the monster scoops him up and carries him to an ancient place where a strange queen leads him into a lake to drown. All this is played out over a gorgeous dizzying array of acoustic instrumentation featuring a killer flute riff and a disarmingly cheery choral sing-along that rounded off an outstanding record ignored by the many but loved by the few, you can tell them by the cheerful twinkle in their eye.

70. Kevin Ayers
The Unfairground
(2007)

So much talent, such good looks, how did Kevin Ayers avoid stardom? The answer to that question is quite clearly that he was repelled by the prospect and as soon as fame seemed feasible he would flee to some Mediterranean bolt hole with plentiful quantities of vino and only re-emerge when the spotlight had shifted.

Kevin was the connoisseurs' choice but never truly popular. His record sales diminished year on year and the half-full venues he performed in grew smaller until by the Nineties and early 2000s when he periodically toured it was the backrooms of pubs before thirty or forty of the faithful; he was going through the motions, disengaged from the whole process, seemingly bewildered by what he was doing and sprinkling just enough magic into the songs to make it worthwhile. It was all more than a little dispiriting and that made the emergence of this classic fifteen years on from his previous studio album such an unexpected delight.

Recorded in New York by an immense cast that included members of Teenage Fanclub, Gorky's Zygotic Minci and Neutral Milk Hotel, as well as contemporaries Hugh Hopper, Phil Manzanera, Bridget St.John and, in sampled form, Robert Wyatt, this was Ayers fully formed and confident. It was a quite wondrous return to the form of his brilliant if largely forgotten Seventies albums. It's an older, wiser, more reflective Ayers than of yore, he's melancholy but not remotely maudlin, his voice has deepened but still the poetry of his words is seemingly delivered as quickly as the thought appears in his head. Love, regrets and ageing are the primary topics dealt with while the arrangements and playing are completely sympathetic – the texture and shading emphasise the richness of the material.

Opening with the jaunty *"Only Heaven Knows"* one could be fooled by how breezy and bright the track sounds that it is celebratory but in truth the singer is laying out his own vulnerability. *"Cold Shoulder"* meditates on loneliness with a lovely backing vocal from Wyatt and a superb string arrangement. *"Walk On Water"* has Ayers' trademark acoustic guitar strum while he sings of mask wearing and superficiality, *"Friends and Strangers"* is an ironic take on relationships over a woozy staggering waltz, *"Brainstorm"* is one of those brooding mini epics at which Ayers has always been adept and reminds me of pieces from his *Confessions of Dr Dream* album in its tone where Manzanera's knack of extracting a remarkable sound from an electric guitar comes to the fore.

Unfairground is, as one would expect, a spin inside a wonky house of horrors while Ayers wittily points out the true darkness around us; *"Run Run Run"* brings to an end one of the great comebacks with its "...your running running away" refrain surely a nod to the author's desire to get back to the blissful quiet life of sunshine and fine wines.

71. Cornershop

Handcream For A Generation (2002)

I remember being told about a pan-Asian punk rock band calling themselves Cornershop and grinning from ear to ear. It was such a glorious subversion of stereotyping, without hearing them I was most definitely onside with them. I noticed David Byrne signed them to his Luka Bop label, I noticed the photograph of them burning a picture of Morrissey for his alleged racism and like the rest of the world I noticed when in remixed form *"Brimfull of Asha"* went to number one on the hit parade sweeping the attendant album into the higher reaches of the charts and I also noticed what reluctant pop stars Cornershop were. The success seemed to be abhorrent to them and off they scuttled to indulge in their dance infused side project Clinton taking four years before returning with this deliberately anti-pop pop album.

What is served up is a feast of grooves underpinning an immersion in styles from multiple locations and cultures with a vaguely psychedelic fuzziness seeping through the whole like brandy in a Christmas cake. Lyric-wise the songs are either nonsensical and the vocals are utilised as another sound in the mix and to provide hooks or they're too obscure for my mind to process coherently. It doesn't matter or spoil my enjoyment though, so rich is the texture and the flavours and so coherently do the pieces flow together despite their differing styles. Nothing is attempted that could be construed as a retread of 'the hit' in fact only *"Staging the Plaguing of the Raised Platform"* which gets away somehow with utilising children cheerfully singing the chorus and *"Lessons Learned from Rocky I to Rocky III"* have the kind of structures beloved of radio programmers, elsewhere there is soul legend Otis Clay MC'ing *"Heavy Soup"*, a Roots Reggae tribute to Lee Perry on *"Motion the 11"*.

There's a post-colonial political dimension apparent throughout, none more than in the provocative Dust Brothers-esque *"Wogs Will Walk"*. The whole premise of *Handcream for a Generation* is an up yours to the formulaic white guitar band-dominated post-Britpop music scene with plentiful funky beats and mirrorball excess contained in this kaleidoscopic uplifting one world disco jamboree.

72. Lynyrd Skynyrd
One More from the Road (1976)

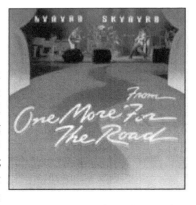

The Southern Rock phenomenon that ran through the Seventies is often derided as gratuitous guitar soloing rednecks who couldn't write songs having a hootenanny; their music too crude for superior tastes. Utter hogwash of course and a view tinged with elitism. Quite often these white boys played with equal amounts of passion and soul as their black Blues and Soul counterparts below the Mason-Dixon line who attracted high praise.

The Allman Brothers Band and Black Oak Arkansas set the ball rolling, but the emergence of Lynyrd Skynyrd in 1973 was when the pulse really quickened, this was a band with the skill of The Allmans and the grit of Black Oak Arkansas but crucially with top notch songs, and lots of them far superior to any of their rival's efforts.

As good as their records were, the true strength of the band was in their live shows where there was an incredible coming together between the performers and audience. They bristled with defiant attitude and poured emotion into their music. Their crowds in the Southern states identified with them because there was no rock star bullshit from Skynyrd, they were interchangeable with the people they met everyday on the street and their music spoke of their lives. Proud of their Southern heritage, they carried that tradition with them and the underdog status that came as part of the package imbued them with a decidedly 'Punk' edge. To attempt to capture this live phenomenon and its atmosphere on record was the task here and I for one am eternally grateful the task was undertaken and achieved.

This was recorded at Atlanta's Fox Theatre over three nights by Tom Dowd and is a stupendous demonstration of the band's ability and the sheer fire-power at their disposal, neither the quality of material or the mix of finesse and fire in their playing falters for even an instant as singer Ronnie Van Zant mixes tenderness with a tough barked growl depending on what's required and even coming from within the grooves of a forty-year-old record he exudes charisma. The three lead guitar attack is breathtaking and never bombastic, while classically-trained pianist Billy Powell remains in a largely supportive role, unobtrusive but crucial to the whole sound. All the big songs are here *"Tuesday's Gone"*, *"Saturday Night Special"*, *"Gimme Three Steps"* the Southern anthem of *"Sweet Home Alabama"* and they all burn white hot! Jimmie Rodgers' *"T is for Texas"* is gleefully rampaged through, Robert Johnson's *"Crossroads"* screams badness, and to top the lot there is an eleven-and-a-half minute *"Freebird"* that takes me to air guitar heaven.

73. Billy Fury
The Sound of Fury
(1960)

From Larry Parnes's stable of largely interchangeable stars Billy Fury emerged as the one true unique talent and the closest thing the UK ever had to a genuine Rock & Roll star to compare with the American founding fathers of the genre. Unfortunately he didn't get to record this debut album until 1960 by which time it was widely assumed that the 'Rock' sound was on the way out to be replaced by the squeaky clean legion of 'Bobbies' who were poised to turn back the tide of the youth explosion in favour of good old family entertainment.

Recorded in one day and released as a ten-inch platter housed in a sleeve showing Billy dressed head to toe in a Gold Lamé suit, looking startled and bequiffed, all ten tracks clock in at around the two minute mark but make what proved to be a remarkable record.

Arranged by pianist Reg Guest from a tape recording of the songs performed on acoustic guitar by Billy, he was joined in the studio by Joe Brown on guitar, Alan White (later the drummer on The Beatles *"Love Me Do"*) and two bass players to ensure a thick sound with some wallop. Alan Weighall on electric and Bill Stark on stand up bass with harmony vocals by a Scottish comedy harmony group The Four Jays, their task was to create a facsimile of the recordings made by Elvis Presley in Sam Phillips' Sun Studios with Reg asked to replicate Floyd Cramer's style and Joe Brown told to do his Scotty Moore impression. Remarkably they achieve this gargantuan feat and more going beyond that by introducing a more Blues influenced feel to proceedings, much credit going to Joe Brown whose playing is wonderfully fluid and versatile as he channels his love of the great Country and Rockabilly guitarists into the overall sound which is always warm and intimate. The songs, all written by Fury, pull in a wide range of influences from Eddie Cochran and Elvis to Johnny Ray and display a burgeoning talent that only a lack of confidence prevented from fully blooming while his singing style is similar to the purr of the great Gene Vincent.

The album was a wondrous accomplishment although it didn't sell well, reaching a high of number eighteen for a solitary week on the chart but any disbelievers that there ever was such a thing as a great British Rock & Roll album should check the slinky *"That's Love"*, the country-styled *"My Advice"* and the moody and atmospheric *"Alright Goodbye"* or the glorious Rockabilly of *"Turn My Back On You"*. *The Sound of Fury* delivers in spades.

74. The Monkees

The Monkees (1966)

The Monkees were the perfectly-timed, manufactured pop band. Just as The Beatles withdrew into their own world and started releasing confusing, sophisticated albums, into the breach stepped four new lovable mop-tops who could be seen having zany fun every week on their television show and whose music was tailored to fill the gap left by their Liverpudlian forebears.

For vibrant upbeat sing-along pop, there was cheerful wacky Micky, cute Davey Jones with his exaggerated English accent, the dreamy Peter and the caustic cerebral Mike in his bobble hat. No wonder the rock crowd, with their obsession with authenticity, dismissed them as fakes and then, as if to add further fuel to the situation, the band themselves let the cat out of the bag that they didn't even play on the records! Shock horror it was all the work of the Wrecking Crew, the studio musicians who played on Phil Spector's string of classics and the Beach Boys' run of hits. For any self-respecting music fan The Monkees were reviled and scorned. They were a huge commercial success but would never be taken seriously, never be considered cool which would have been fine except of course they wanted to be cool and serious and as they became more powerful and emboldened were able to add their own subversive twist to the tale but that came later in their story, this was their first album with much riding on it, would it be popular? Would it sell? The answer to those questions was a resounding "yes" but was it any good? Half a century later, does it pass muster or is it really the empty vessel that the cool cats perceived it to be? In my humble opinion it was an excellent album in 1967 and in the here and now is still a hugely enjoyable and vibrant listen.

Wisely the bulk of the lead singing is handed to Micky Dolenz who was a truly great vocalist capable of extracting the maximum amount of zip from each phrase. The more whimsical and lightweight Davy Jones gets two songs and Mike Nesmith not only sings the two songs he was allowed to write but produced them and features Peter Tork playing guitar. Tommy Boyce and Bobby Hart produce the rest of the album and write the majority of the songs with Gerry Goffin and Carole King chipping in, all the material except the closing *"Gonna Buy Me a Dog"* which tries too hard to be funny but ends up just silly, are great pop tunes with a bubblegum/garage sound that is exhilaratingly full of life. Surprisingly only one single was extracted from the album, the still thrilling *"Last Train to Clarksville"* which gave the band their first hit. Other great tracks are *"(Theme From) The Monkees"* which is a transportive trip to happy childhood days for myself and I suspect many others. *"Take a Giant Step"*, *"Tomorrow's Gonna Be Another Day"* and *"I Wanna Be Free"* all are Pop magic and *"Sweet Young Thing"* written by Nesmith with Goffin and King is quite stunningly original in its use of spiralling guitars and fiddles.

It was an exploitative and brazenly 'in it for the money' exercise that was hugely profitable for the creators of The Monkees but regardless of whether by accident or design, the undeniable truth is that brilliant music was a by-product of the enterprise and this was exhibit A in support of that statement.

75. T. Rex

Futuristic Dragon (1976)

By the time this album was released in January 1976 Marc Bolan and T. Rex had been in the wilderness for the best part of three years, deserted by the majority of their legion of fans from the 1970 to 1972 heyday, Bolan had piled on the pounds, his elfin features as bloated as his ego. A Napoleon complex, apparently fuelled by cocaine addiction, and antagonised by a once adoring press who aimed cruel jibes at the ex-star whenever he was mentioned. He was the epitome of the burned out, washed up Rock Star.

The arrival of David Bowie and Roxy Music had knocked him from his perch and made him sound old. He'd tried to keep up, but simply didn't have it in him and had lost sight of what made him great in the first place as he chased new sounds that didn't suit him. *Futuristic Dragon* was the start of his renaissance. Fortified by the numbers who turned out to see him on tour, he realised all was not lost and began recording this new album, this new start. The songs were less convoluted with stronger riffs than any he'd released for years and his lyrics were as audacious and as silly as those that had wowed us when he kick-started the Seventies.

In as much of a thrall to Soul and Disco as Rock & Roll, many of the grooves the songs ride on are based on soulful rhythms while the orchestration owes much to the influence of Barry White. The record is notable for its full sound, no other *T. Rex* recordings have this audible density. The record kicks off with a squall of screaming guitar noise with Marc donning his poets cap to recite baffling verse to us; it is perhaps a stylistic nod to *"Future Legend"* the track with which Bowie had opened *Diamond Dogs*. It's not as successful but *"Jupiter Liar"* which follows is a crunching winner, upbeat and a real return to form. *"Chrome Sitar"* is even better mid-paced and benefiting from a superb backing vocal from Gloria Jones. *"All Alone"* would have sat quite comfortably on *Slider* which is praise enough and is followed by *"New York City"* a genuine hit single where you feel all the old magic and confidence return as the preposterous tale of seeing a "...woman coming out of New York City with a frog in her hand" plays out over piano, sax, strings and gospel backing vocals. *"Calling All Destroyers"* is one of the great T. Rex tracks and very proto-punk in its energy and madcap effervescence. *"Theme for a Dragon"* is a strange hybrid of a Philly Soul sound instrumental track and a hysterical crowd screaming over the top; bizarre but on a T. Rex album the bizarre has its place. *"Dreamy Lady"*, another hit single, is a floating Disco piece with Marc cast as mystical thinking Lothario. *"Casual Agent"* closes the record in fine style and reaffirmed, at least to the faithful, that Bolan was back.

76. Imagination

Body Talk (1981)

This debut from Imagination was probably the most forward-looking pop album of the 1980s. Though at the time they were barely taken seriously, little credibility was given to their work and much more attention was focussed on their homoerotic appearance which one has to concede was highly striking.

They came together when singer/keyboard player Leee John,

who worked as a supporting player for the likes of the Delfonics and Chairman of the Board, struck up a musical partnership with guitarist/bassist Ashley Ingram. They worked on creating slinky soulful erotic music forming a short lived band called Fizzz before a meeting with drummer Errol Kennedy of Brit funk band TFB completed the line up. They approached production team Swain and Jolley, who had worked with Irish singer Joe Dolan, it was a bizarre choice but proved to be hugely inspired.

The title track from the album became an instant hit when released as a single and revealed an innovative new sound of soul. It was unusually British sounding when the accepted mode within the genre was to ape what came from the States. Here everything was played slow and simple with unchanging rhythms decorated by piano trills and synthesiser swells; the vocals sweet, seductive and sultry floated over this divine backing never straining to be heard, never rushed, key phrases repeated over and over creating insidious ear worms – this was minimalist perfection. The teasing shimmer of *"Body Talk"* opens the album superbly giving way to the slightly brisker *"So Good, So Right"* which is seven minutes of an exotic unveiling that is absolutely delicious. *"Burnin' Up"* is the album's crowning masterpiece, hugely influential on the Chicago House scene Marshall Jefferson's classic *"Move Your Body"* could never have existed without it. Two more hits follow; *"Flashback"* and *"In and Out of Love"* both gorgeous dancefloor-filling gems as well as the even slower than the rest of the album *"I'll Always Love You (But Don't Look Back)"* to complete a near flawless album that owed nothing to the rule book but all to inspiration and imagination.

77. The Auteurs

After Murder Park

(1996)

Peaking commercially when their first album was nominated for the Mercury Prize and lumped in with the gathering Brit-pop pack, Auteurs' singer/ songwriter Luke Haines seemed hell-bent on distancing himself from the vapid cocaine-fuelled celebrity of his glamour-obsessed peers, going as far as fantasising on this album's *"Tombstone"* of blowing up the Columbia hotel name-checked by the ghastly Oasis where the new rock star elite hung out.

This third album was a decidedly anti-Britpop statement from its subject matter of destructive behaviour ranging from spousal abuse to child murder and, in the choice of Steve Albini as producer, to provide a vicious unfriendly guitar and cello sound alongside mournful organ and a creepy claustrophobic atmosphere throughout, Haines' lyrics paint places and situations where unpleasantness is not merely hinted at but laid bare and dissected and where painful memories do not abate.

"...When you cut a lover slack you'll get a fucking monster back" is the opening line of the opening song *"Light Aircraft on Fire"* which sets the mood in startling style. The aircraft in question is a metaphor for a relationship ready to crash in spectacular fashion. Haines hisses and whispers his way through *"Child Brides"* over a near funereal dirge. *"Land Lovers"* with its winning violin riffing and tempo changes is reminiscent of those other under appreciated, hugely literary thinking person's popsters The Go Betweens. *"New Brat in Town"* possibly aimed at Damon, Liam and Noel is a growling slab of malevolence.

The centrepiece of the album is undoubtedly *"Unsolved Child*

Murder" in which Haines remembers a dark incident from his own childhood over an *"Eleanor Rigby"*-like stringed backdrop. More messy personal lives are examined on *"Married to a Lazy Lover"*, the rancorous and misogynistic tone without a happy ending. Fortunately one of the albums few cheery moments is looming where on *"Buddha"* Haines sings a refrain of "...Buddha , Buddha , Buddha Whoo!" amid the misery and carnage. *"Fear of Flying"* seems to be about underachieving and displays a degree of tenderness, *"Dead Sea Navigators"* is disarmingly harmonious upon the surface but the refrain of "...one of us is crazy and I think that it's you..." illustrates the song's darker heart.

Sales were dismal, which is perhaps unsurprising given the climate of cheery optimism and bullish self-belief of Brit Pop – who wanted confronting with discomforting home truths? There was only one more Auteurs album to come, the excellent *How I Learned to Love the Bootboys* but Haines has regularly released albums in a variety of guises, all of them are high quality and refreshingly free of sops aimed at acceptability but if I were to choose one of his records to accompany me on a lone sabbatical it would undoubtedly be *After Murder Park*.

78. Mungo Jerry
Electronically Tested
(1971)

Ray Dorset and Colin Earl had been members of a late Sixties band called Good Earth who, on sacking their inept drummer decided to proceed without one, instead using stamped feet or a washboard as a rhythmic device as they gravitated in a Folk-Blues Jugband direction.

They made their debut as a four-piece using the name Mungo

Jerry for the first time at the Hollywood Festival in Staffordshire alongside Black Sabbath, Traffic and The Grateful Dead in early summer 1970. They stole the show, their good time stage act and lack of pretension endearing them to an audience ready to have fun. The next week their single *"In the Summertime"* went into the charts, a week later it was number one and seemed to stay there until autumn leaves began to fall.

"We're not grey people , we're not dirty or mean, we love everybody but we do as we please…" ran part of the lyric and it chimed perfectly with the times. Headlines soon proclaimed the arrival of *"Mungomania"*, although it's doubtful Marc Bolan was shaking in his pretty ladies shoes. Still the next single, the extremely near to the knuckle *"Baby Jump",* went to number one and the one that followed "*Lady Rose*" was only prevented from repeating the feat when the BBC took umbrage at the B side *"Have a Whiff on Me"* which advocated cocaine use and banned it from the airwaves. In the midst of this *Electronically Tested,* their second album followed, cheekily pinching the slogan used to endorse the nation's biggest selling brand of condoms as its title.

Electronically Tested is such a brilliant record that it's difficult to understand how it has grown to be so neglected. With a front cover image of the band being rapturously received at their breakthrough gig at the Hollywood Festival indicating that within we would find excitement and entertainment, *"She Rowed"* kicks the album off in what can only be described as storming fashion with this loose-limbed shuffle with an infectious chorus. Next, a nine minute take on Willie Dixon's *"I Just Wanna Make Love to You"* never sags or feels like it's overstaying its welcome and is in turn followed by *"In the Summertime".* Far from politically correct when viewed with the benefit of hindsight, it remains as catchy as hellfire and despite the best part of a half a century's over-exposure it still raises a smile; it's good time music at its finest. *"Somebody Stole My Wife",* later released as a single, is the closing track on side one and another rollicking stomp. The thrilling *"Baby Jump"* starts side two in frenzied Jerry Lee Lewis style and a leering vocal from Ray Dorset is perfectly suitable for this lewdist of lewd rockers, *"Memoirs of a*

Stockbroker" is almost Kinks-like in its eccentricity and the world weary and resigned *"Coming Back to You When the Time Comes"* show that Dorset had more strings to his bow than the hedonistic odes that were his stock-in-trade.

Things took a turn for the strange not many months later down the line when Colin Earl and Paul King approached the record company with the proposal that Dorset be replaced. Horrified at the prospect, the label instead fired them. Mungo Jerry was split in two. Dorset recruited a more conventional line up and until 1976 the hits continued without ever containing any of the wow factor that make this such a brilliant record.

79. Laura Nyro
Eli and the Thirteenth Confession (1968)

Laura Nyro was treated appallingly by the music critics of the day; if they weren't outright hostile and negative they were patronising and constantly harped on about the shrillness of her voice, was it simply that they felt threatened? Could it be that in the male-dominated music scene of the Sixties a woman so talented, uncompromising and creative was not what was expected. Here was a twenty-year-old woman who didn't have a man behind the scenes telling her what to do and how to act. Laura had already walked out of one record contract citing interference while recording her first album. For this, her second album, she would have complete control.

From a basic classic Pop sound elements of Soul, Jazz, Folk and Broadway show tunes go to make up the rich musical tapestry of the album whilst lyrically the strongest motifs are love and death. The album is fully formed, which is remarkable for one so young and blazed a creative trail that eased the way for the likes of Joni

Mitchell and Rickie Lee Jones and inspired and influenced Todd Rundgren and Elton John.

Starting in unapologetically exuberant style; *"Luckie"*, *"Lu"* and *"Sweet Blindness"* are a 1-2-3 combination that display the gifts of the artist to the full. Powerful, passionate vocals and songs with a real sense of drama are wonderfully arranged and imaginatively played utilising Laura's prowess as pianist supplemented by Jazz guitars, vibes and flutes as well as gospel-flavoured backing vocals. *"Poverty Train"* introduces a Blues feel to the record and is utterly compelling followed by the even bluesier *"Lonely Women"* featuring a smokey coiling saxophone while side one closer *"Eli's Coming"* has a beautiful Hammond organ intro giving way to a push and pull rhythm and call and response vocals that take the song into feverish abandon before the gentle warning refrain of *"...Eli's coming, better hide your heart"* closes out the song.

Side two begins with *"Timer"* a mid-tempo piano-led joy, followed by *"Stone Soul Picnic"* a light and airy delight made a fine hit single when 'normalised' by The 5th Dimension. *"Emmie"* is sweet and quite gorgeous while stretching out over long horn notes *"Woman's Blues"* gives way to a funky drum beat, *"Once It Was Alright (Farmer Joe)"* is a shape-shifting classic of audacity and wit, *"December's Boudoir"* and *"The Confession"* are the closing tracks; the first as delicate as a snowflake and perhaps an inspiration to Kate Bush in her winter-themed work, the second a precursor to what Joni Mitchell's sound would evolve into as the acoustic guitar at the centre of the piece is supported by sundry percussion devices and horns.

80. Howard Tate
Get it While You Can (1966)

When people talk about the great writer/producers of Sixties Soul, they usually reference the Hayes/Porter team at Stax or Holland/Dozier/Holland at Motown alongside the likes of Van McCoy, Curtis Mayfield and the team of Dan Penn and Chips Moman. Few will mention Jerry Ragovoy, despite him conjuring up among others *"Stay With Me Baby"* for Lorraine Ellison and *"Time is on My Side"* for Irma Thomas. Likewise, discuss the great Soul voices of the era and Aretha, Otis, Marvin, Sam Cooke, Jackie Wilson and James Carr will instantly spring to mind but probably not Howard Tate who was every bit their equal and whose album *Get it While You Can* should be rated just as highly as *Otis Blue, Live at the Apollo* or *Lady Soul* as landmarks of the genre.

Ragovoy heard Howard Tate singing as part of Garnet Mimms' band The Gainors and, struck by his voice, tracked him down to cut some solo material. Tate, like James Brown, was born in Macon, Georgia although he moved to Philadelphia as a child. His voice was powerful and within his range was a stunning falsetto but his greatest gift was not his impeccable technique but his ability to transmit what he sang on an emotional level.

His second single *"Ain't Nobody Home"* had been a number 67 American hit and browsing through racks of records as was my want at some point in the mid-Seventies, I chanced upon it and although I wasn't familiar with it, I purchased it due to Jerry Ragovoy being on the credits. I was captivated by its easy conversational tone and the feel of the performance. No grandstanding was necessary, it simply oozed real Soul. A week later I located this album and I was expecting to find perhaps a few good cuts mixed in with lots of filler. I couldn't have been more wrong; from top to bottom this was absolute dynamite.

Beginning with the single and then onto a superb guitar-led soul blues on *"Part Time Love"* a Mod Jazz organ propelled *"Glad I Knew Better"* before more horn-driven Blues on *"How Blue Can You Get?"* these are all magnificent recordings but the album title track topped the lot. *"Get it While You Can"* is simply one of the absolute great Soul recordings. A reading of the Joe Williams standard *"Everyday I Have the Blues"* is tackled with such authority that it becomes the definitive version. *"How Come My Bulldog Don't Bark"* is wryly humorous and ironic, though never crosses the line into novelty territory and *"Look at Granny Run Run"* is a fine strutting closer in Stax Records style with funk guitar and a crescendo of horns accompanying a vocal full of warmth and gleeful good humour. Janis Joplin and Jimi Hendrix plucked material from the album which showed impeccable good taste but it wasn't the big seller it deserved to be.

By the early Eighties, Howard Tate had disappeared following the tragic death of his thirteen-year-old daughter in a house fire. Drug addicted and staying in a homeless shelter he eventually rallied and found work counselling drug abusers and people suffering from poor mental health. After a decade long search Jerry Ragovoy discovered his whereabouts and contacted him leading to them recording together again and releasing the 2003 album *Rediscovered*.

81. ELP
Trilogy (1972)

The ultimate whipping boys for the sins of prog excess and a supergroup to boot, it's not always been easy to defend my fondness for ELP and I have not been immune to self-doubt not least after seeing them perform at Manchester's Hardrock in the year of this release, one of the most excruciatingly boring nights of my life as they played for three whole hours, though it seemed much longer, smugly basking in the adulation of an audience sat uncomfortably cross-legged in pretentious idiocy. That memory kept their albums, which had been listening staples, off my turntable for a long period. But when I tentatively gave them a second chance I found myself hooked again on this album in particular.

Emerson, Lake and Palmer had come together in 1970, refugees from The Nice, King Crimson and Atomic Rooster respectively. They were big news from their inception and had soon built up a huge fan base on both sides of the Atlantic. However their previous album had caused a rift between Keith Emerson, who was pushing the music in a dense bombastic direction, and Greg Lake who was vocal in his dislike for the material. A split looked likely but was averted by the band's management acting as mediators. The enormous success of *Tarkus* must have been bittersweet for Greg Lake, nonetheless his criticism seemed to have been heeded when *Trilogy* was released as it was revealed to be much more varied than its predecessor, more song-based and with a much lighter touch, it was also much better.

The opening *"The Endless Enigma (Part 1)"* begins with Lake playing low bass notes to replicate a heartbeat before a yearning keyboard motif. A piano run and eastern flavoured drums lead into a brilliantly imaginative piece. Preposterous: yes; full of its own self-importance: yes; but also extremely adventurous and entertaining. *"Fugue",* a beautiful piano piece, separates part 1 of *"Endless Enigma"* from part 2 which in turns evokes a pastoral idyll and the awakening of humankind. Greg Lake's acoustic "*From the Beginning*" adds to the diversity and became an American hit single, perfect as it was for the times in its gorgeous melody and questioning tone. *"The Sheriff"* opens with a drum solo and a wonderful moment where Carl Palmer is heard to exclaim "shit!" as he hits the rim of a tom tom. The song kicks in and is concluded by a honky-tonk piano part with pistols shooting. Aaron Copland's 1942 classical piece *'"Hoedown"* is covered next and given similar thrilling treatment as was meted out to Bernstein's *"America"* by Emerson in his days with The Nice. *"Living Sin"* is the nearest thing to a conventional rock piece before another classic is tackled this time *"Abbadon's Bolero"* its 3/4 time replaced by 4/4 to make the piece sound like a very ominous March rather than a Bolero. The drums are unfaltering as layer upon layer of keyboards are added creating a tension you feel must snap, it's like heading into a battle with blood pumping, nerves on edge and then a dead stop as that moment arrives concludes both the track and one of the essential albums of the Prog era.

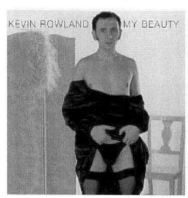

82. Kevin Rowland

My Beauty

(1999)

In the eleven years that had followed Rowland's *The Wanderer,* his Deodato produced solo album, the ex-Dexy's Midnight Runners leader, who had enjoyed huge fame and success in the early Eighties, had been through the wringer; homeless, bankrupt, addicted and struggling to find a meaningful purpose in his life he was no longer "searching for the young soul rebels" but soul searching and striving to correct mistakes. This album comes from that dark place, the songs on this album are what comforted and gave strength to him during that desperate time and because of that they are delivered here with true sincerity and imbued with great poignancy.

This album was released by über-fan Alan McGee's Creation Records. Oasis aside, Creation were a label of exquisite good taste and brave enough to stick to their guns when faced with the inevitable flack this album was bound to attract. From the totally unhip selection of songs to the sleeve art showing a semi-naked Rowland wearing a pearl necklace, women's clothes and underwear and heavily made-up gazing out dolefully before a pink screen.

My Beauty kicks-off with the George Benson hit *"The Greatest Love Of All"* with lyrics altered to personalise the song that reflected the struggles the singer had been through. It is beautifully delivered "...no matter what they say about me - they can't take my personal dignity" states Rowland and clearly this record was a huge step towards rehabilitation. *"Rag Doll"* is given a slower treatment with gospel backing accentuating the sadness of the lyric and is handled impeccably by Rowland. *"Concrete and Clay"* and *"Daydream*

Believer" both sparkle, the former featuring a delicious Spanish guitar break. *"The Guy's In Love With You"* is spare and Jazz-tinged, displaying Rowland's remarkable gift for phrasing that displays the depth within the lyrics. *"It's Getting Better"* in the context of the album is heart-warming. The take on the neglected classic that is The Marmalade's *"Reflections Of My Life"* is full of pathos and pulls heavily on the heartstrings, it is very beautiful. The closer "*You'll Never Walk Alone"* is delivered understatedly, prayer-like, a lifebuoy to cling onto in deep dangerous waters.

There was a long way for Rowland to travel to fully get his life back on track. He would face huge ridicule, and was hauled over the coals in print in the British music press. The gender presentation questioned as being a mid-life crisis forced Alan McGee's office to issue a lengthy statement defending 'the look'. Performing at the Reading Festival to promote this record he faced a barrage of bottles thrown from a baying mob. Then he disappeared from public view once more before staging something of a triumphant return, but none of that would have been possible without the exorcising of demons that took place on this great album.

83. Robert Calvert
Lucky Leif and the Longships
(1975)

Robert Calvert was a fiercely driven creative soul who embraced poetry, theatricality and, after becoming acquainted with Dave Brock of Hawkwind, music. He went on to become lyricist and sometime front man for Brock's band of psychedelic warlords introducing the concepts that fuelled their brand of Space Rock and writing *"Silver Machine"* the hit single that established the band. In 1974 he released his first solo album *Captain Lockheed and the Starfighters,* a concept album inspired by Calvert's childhood dream of becoming a fighter pilot. Among the personnel on that album had been luminaries such as Arthur Brown, Viv Stanshall and Brian Eno playing keyboards. Twelve months later came this album, another conceptual piece, this time produced by Eno for the first time in what would prove to be a stellar career. On board for recording were ex-Pink Fairy Paul Rudolph, Hawkwind violinist Simon House and saxophonist Nik Turner as well as esteemed science fiction author Michael Moorcock on banjo.

The concept the songs were to illustrate was the Viking discovery of the Americas in the 10th century and what would have been the outcome had they colonised the new continent 500 years before Christopher Columbus arrived in 1492. He seems to conclude much the same, but has a lot of fun reaching that conclusion marrying references to the America we know with others. Full of pagan Norse imagery the pick of the bunch coming on a *Beach Boys* parody *"The Lay of the Surfers"* with a chorus of "… Ba Ba Barbarian". The sound mixes the hard rock of Hawkwind with the glam of Roxy Music with excursions into Reggae and the cosmic sludge of Amon Duul and was much criticised for its lack of continuity as the music takes flying leaps here and there. Calvert was happy to declare that Eno was the best possible producer he could have had for this project. His constituent audience of Hawkwind fans were much less happy with an album of tight short songs rather than long jams, it was too strange for them and has consequently been erased from history.

Starting with the sound of Viking horns *"Ship of Fools"* begins the journey and would have slipped seamlessly onto either of Eno's first two solo albums. The aforementioned *"Lay of the Surfers"* follows and by now more narrow-minded listeners were furiously wrenching the needle from the record missing out on the electronic Glam-Folk styled *"Voyaging to Vinland"* which is quite lovely and the strange melding of voices that is *"The Making of Midgard"* there is the piano balladeering of *"Brave New World"* the Blues shuffle with charmingly eccentric vocals of *"Magic Potion"* while the nearest thing to a crowd-pleaser is *"Volstead O Vodeo Do"* with a snaking guitar motif, chanted vocals, it is a strange track but at least recognisably strange for those wondering what's going on. The magpie-like pilfering takes us into Reggae with absolutely no attempt to sound authentic but simply to add colour and further flavour before the final track *"Ragna Rock"* heralds the end of this marvellous oddity of an album with an up-tempo romp and a lyric of vivid imagination.

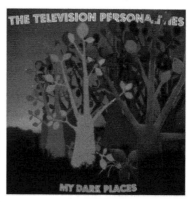

84. Television Personalities

My Dark Places (2006)

When the *Television Personalities* appeared in the late Seventies both parodying and partaking in the Punk scene as it changed to Post-Punk, they were fabulously refreshing. Utterly shambolic and without a trace of macho rock star posturing evident even in the new wave of bands such as Sex Pistols and The Clash, their songs, written by Dan Treacy, were sharp enough to lacerate the pomposity of his targets revealing the ridiculous conceits used as camouflage by those they lampooned but they were delivered with such sweet good-natured charm that they were impossible not to love and yet, there was always a fragility that hinted at a worrying instability. Regular record releases throughout the Eighties attested to the singular talent of Dan Treacy and their influence spread way beyond the fairly minuscule sales, without doubt there was some kind of genius in the grooves of Television Personalities records which seemed to combine elements of The Kinks' and Syd Barrett's song craft.

As the Eighties gave way to the Nineties, Dan Treacy disappeared from sight amid some wild speculation. The truth was the instability brought on by mental illness and heroin addiction had precipitated a downward spiral that resulted in his incarceration on a prison ship. On release he revealed to friends he had been writing songs throughout this period, provided with musical instruments and support. Quickly a record deal was procured and after an absence of eight years a new Television Personalities album crept out into the world.

The first thing that needs to be said is that what is offered up on this album makes for uncomfortable and sometimes harrowing listening. Cut with moments of tender beauty, it is a remarkable look into the troubled soul of its creator. *"Special Chair"* which begins the album is a sad and bitter confessional mixed with barely concealed rage, *"All the Young Children On Smack"* is a spare piece indeed with a beatbox and handclap accompaniment to Treacy's stream of consciousness rambling. *"Sick Again"* pulls no punches either as the singer lays on the line his recurring woes "...I lost the plot" he sadly informs us. *"Ex-Girlfriend Club"* finds Treacy acting as host in said establishment singing a snatch of *"Uptown Top Ranking"* and inviting us to partake of the salad bar. *"Dream The Sweetest Dream"* though shot through with sadness is nonetheless possessed of a fragile loveliness. In *"Velvet Underground"* Dan ponders on the mystery of the titular band's sound as a jaunty romp and its good humour is most welcome. *"My Dark Places"*, *"I'm Not Your Typical Boy"* and *"You Kept Me Waiting Too Long"* are fully realised pieces, achingly sad but still glorious. *"They'll Have To Catch Us First"* is simply a cheerful interlude seemingly thrown together. It leads us to *"She Can Stop Traffic"* which is a cheery groover of the highest order full of the charm associated with The Television Personalities. *"Tell Me About Your Day"* is a wistful piano piece before the deeply sad *"Then a Big Boy Came and Knocked It All Down"* where the pain of being bullied at school and the effects of that bullying are spelt out over a funereal organ. *"I Hope You're Happy Now"* is more wistful, reminiscing on a lost love. *"No More I Hate You's"* continues the theme of love gone wrong and the closing track *"There's No Beautiful Way To Say Goodbye"* is aching with a brittle-voiced Dan Treacy wrestling with more despair.

Serious illness following brain surgery in 2011 has silenced Dan Treacy although in 2016 his family reported he was improving and wanted to make music again, I most sincerely hope that comes to pass.

85. The Residents
Eskimo (1979)

The Residents, like The Ramones, are appreciated more for the iconography of image rather than the startling music they made. Beyond devoted fans, *Eskimo* is the record which frightens casual listeners most with its chilling atmosphere, incomprehensible chanting and almost total lack of rhythm, it is considered too far out and unfriendly for most people's tastes.

What they miss of course is The Residents mischievous sense of fun, even though the supposed subject matter here is serious, concerning as it does the assimilation of an ancient people into the modern commercialised world, the approach is playful rather than pretentious and though they may seem obscure, there are jokes aplenty inside this splendidly different album.

The recording of *Eskimo* began in early summer 1976. The Residents having made their Punk Statement with a deconstructed version of The Rolling Stones *"I Can't Get No Satisfaction"*, were set to move on and examine the Arctic and its culture through musical ethnic forgery. The story told on the sleeve of the album purports to be a historically accurate document of "Inuit life" in the Arctic Circle but is in truth a deliberately far-fetched fiction with no more than a kernel of authenticity contained within it and the "Eskimo" chanting that runs throughout the album is mostly an almost indescribable mix of gibberish and slogans satirising the commercial world's hard sell. The band themselves were unsure if they hadn't gone too far towards pretentiousness, losing the purity of the original idea and laboured on the recording on and off for close to three years - they needn't have worried because *Eskimo* is in my opinion their crowning achievement.

Though split into six tracks, the album is best digested as one hugely atmospheric piece. Opening with mournful low horns and a synthesised wind that blows throughout the album, there is the chatter of the indigenous people clinging to their existence in an ever-hostile environment. A brighter section evoking the sun over great swathes of ice breaks into a rhythmic chant and then a deep lone voice accompanied by a screeching infant. Some homemade stringed instrument is plucked over a yearning lament that may well be extolling the virtue of "Coca Cola is Life" but by now the album notes are abandoned and I close my eyes and follow this imaginary journey unaided but for my own imagination. On we travel through this Arctic wasteland, the swirling wind ever present and the indigenous people trekking if as one carried by their spirit and fortitude. The music unfolds and one can't help but feel astonishment at The Residents achievement in this creation; the bravado, audacity and originality of approach is unrivalled even among their own work, making *Eskimo* an album that really has to be heard and experienced.

86. Neil Diamond
Hot August Night
(1972)

Secondhand shops around the globe are full of copies of this huge selling but unloved artefact that encapsulates a time and a place when Neil Diamond was a huge star.

It is not a flawless masterpiece and several of Diamond's studio albums are of superior quality but here, spread over four glorious sides, is Neil as icon. Having left his collar and tie and short hair behind when he stepped out of the famed Brill Building where he had crafted brilliant pop hits for The Monkees, he started having hits of his own and soon became a star. Now he wanted to go beyond that and wanted superstar status, he also wanted respect and credibility and to that end he quit New York for life amongst the hip rock elite in Los Angeles. A live double album was almost a prerequisite for acceptance into that club and *Hot August Night* is lavishly packaged with a front cover of Neil in body-hugging double denim "pantomiming whanging his clanger" as Lester Bangs put it in his *Rolling Stone* magazine review. It was a strategic marketing move to align Neil with those who breathed the rarefied air of both critical favour and huge commercial success. Neil wanted what Bob Dylan had, what Carole King had, what The Band had and this epic album, full of grandeur and pretentiousness as well as superlative music, was his ace card.

Recorded as part of a sold-out run at LA's Greek Theatre with band and full orchestra accompanying him, Neil enters after a three minute orchestral introduction that seems to last much longer, before going into the rocking *"Crunchy Granola"*. From the off, the performance is overwrought; straining to wring emotion out of every line. It's more pompous and bombastic than Elvis ever was in his Vegas era but this marriage of old-style entertainment and a rocker sensibility is somehow satisfying, perhaps because in truth the two are one and the same. There are cornball passages of scripted dialogue where Neil attempts to pass himself off as a light-hearted joker, which he clearly is not, and there are a couple of embarrassing dreadful songs in *"Soggy Pretzels"* and *"Porcupine Pie"*, but against that there is material that is timeless being performed with passion and absolute conviction and the combination brings clarity and fullness to proceedings while it captures the ebb and flow that makes a live show so exhilarating. Those great songs too, who can resist *"Cherry Cherry"*, *"Red Red Wine"*, *"Girl, You'll Be a Woman Soon"*, *"Sweet Caroline"*, *"Song Sung Blue"*, *"I Am…I Said"*, *"Cracklin' Rosie"* before the the show and album are brought to a close with a hysterical *"Brother Love's Travelling Salvation Show"*.

87. The Go-Betweens

Oceans Apart 2005)

the go-betweens oceans apart

Formed in 1977 around the talents of song writers Grant McLennan and Robert Forster, who remained the only constants in the band, The Go-Betweens ever-shifting line-up survived until 1989 on extremely meagre commercial pickings. Drummer Lindy Morrison later declared, "No one ever cared except a handful of wanky journalists and some students", not quite true, I loved them with all my heart but you get the picture.

When they called time on the band it was like putting a bullet into a faithful old horse turned lame. It was a mercy killing and it was time to explore other avenues, there was sadness and a sense of loss but they had left behind six remarkable albums that left an indelible impression on those of us who admired them. They left memories of great shows where, without fuss, they performed brilliant song after brilliant song.

In the year 2000, McLennan and Forster reunited as The Go-Betweens with a new set of musicians to play alongside. Reunions and revivals were all the rage as artistically bankrupt aggregations reformed to cash-in on the vogue for nostalgia – it was and remains an unedifying spectacle, yet there was not a hint of cynicism about The Go-Betweens coming together once more, there was a sense of unfinished business and much was left to say now that batteries had been recharged.

This was the third album of the band's second coming, the first two had been shot through with brilliance but were undermined by a lack of confidence. They sounded tentative as they worked towards relocating their magical chemistry. Here they found it, bringing in producer Mark Wallis who had done a brilliant job on the classic *16 Lovers Lane* was a wise move, he understood the band

and sought to bring out the textures and nuances that had become hidden, he added more colour with more prominent keyboards and electric percussion. McLennan and Forster too were armed with a clutch of excellent songs, their contrasting approaches to writing complimenting one another; the former reflective and soulful, the latter sharp, angular and a master of word play.

The first of the ten tracks, Forster's *"Here Comes the City"*, is a superb evocation of travel and travels on a sprightly riff while Forster's slightly detached vocal, every syllable enunciated with precision, is arresting. McLennan's *"Finding You"* follows and again travel is a motif but here the wistfulness and bewilderment of the singer are evident as the song flows then swells like a dam of emotion ready to burst, and so the album progresses never losing momentum or lessening in quality making it among the very finest of the band's catalogue. *"Darlinghurst Nights"*, with its use of horns, is a wonderful track as is the achingly beautiful title track that is full of questions and a longing that aches. The marvellous album centrepiece *"The Statue"* is a shimmering melodic masterpiece, Forster closes the album with *"The Mountains Near Dellray"* in suitably understated mysterious fashion rounding off what was to be the final Go-Betweens album in superlative style.

88. Bim Sherman
Miracle (1996)

Bim Sherman, or Jarret Lloyd Vincent to give him his birth name, cut some high quality, though obscure, Roots Reggae sides in Jamaica before uprooting and joining the ranks of the quite superlative On-U-Sound label helmed by producer extraordinaire Adrian Maxwell. Sherman appeared on records alongside the likes of Ari Up and Prince Far I by outfits New Age Steppers and Singers and Players before recording this experimental genre-melding semi forgotten classic under his own name.

What is served up is an unplugged Reggae album that is drumless, thus rendering it not really Reggae, combined with an Eastern flavour topped by Sherman's extraordinarily beautiful voice which is honey-coated and impossibly sweet. Maxwell produces impeccably; restraining his instincts for studio trickery, while On-U-Sound stalwarts Doug Wimbish, on very tasteful bass, and Skip McDonald on acoustic guitar, support alongside a young Talvin Singh on Tabla and the strings of the Studio Beats Orchestra of Bombay, to create a gentle rolling soundscape of layered textures that is remarkable. Sherman writes or co-writes ten of the eleven tracks. There are some re-recordings of his Jamaican releases and some new recordings while the one cover, *"Bewildered"*, fits perfectly.

The recycled *"Golden Locks"* is track one, "...look at those beautiful black locks, don't you realise they are gold?" sings Sherman and the listener is transported into a world of beauty and liquid gold. If there is a heaven then this surely is the soundtrack. There is a Zen calm throughout the record and though never preachy, a real sense of spirituality is imparted even as the singer addresses earthly concerns such as on "Can I Be Free From Crying" where he seems to be addressing his question to a higher, wiser watcher. Each track seems to replicate the soulfulness of the previous one. One song after the other maintains the quality of its predecessor making this a blissfully soothing, meditative trip of an album without any of the blandness of the "Chill out" and "New Age" genres. Think of this rather as a fellow traveller in the direction Massive Attack and Portishead would take; slowing down the pace, adding a cinematic feel and utilising distinctive voices capable of expressing real emotion.

89. Bill Withers

Still Bill

(1972)

Bill Withers has somehow become the forgotten giant of Seventies Soul, even though his records were big sellers and found critical favour he was never revered in the way Marvin, Curtis or Stevie, were, and still are. Perhaps it is because his records sound simple and unadorned, reflecting his refreshing down to earth attitude and blue collar roots but listen a few times and his songs reveal timeless melodies and lyrically he was certainly a better writer than his peers. There was unadorned honesty in his words, as well as a knack of tackling complexities in everyday language, maybe it's because he wasn't as easy to categorise as an out-and-out Soul man as others because his music contained strong elements of the Blues and Folk based singer-songwriter genres. Whatever the reason, it is hugely regrettable that the memory of Bill Withers golden streak of classic Seventies album have been forgotten. He was a uniquely gifted man whose music was as uplifting as it was individualistic.

Coming a year after his debut album, *Just As I Am, Still Bill* was produced by Booker T Jones who had discovered him working at an aeroplane seat manufacturers. For this follow-up, Booker T was unavailable so he went in using the musicians he'd been touring with, the esteemed 103rd Street Rhythm Band. What they produced was an even funkier record than that classic which had contained gems like *"Grandma's Hands"* and *"Ain't No Sunshine"*. This one matches the high strike rate with the Gospel infused *"Lean On Me"* featuring one of the most exquisitely tasteful vocal performances we are likely to hear. There is no grandstanding, no wringing the lyric of emotion, just straight, restrained and subtle which gives the epic chorus so much power. The other hit *"Use Me"* might just be the most honest and adult song written about sex and submission to another's desires. *"Who Is He (And What Is He To You)?"* is a genius song of deep jealousy that features a desperately funky wah-wah guitar that positively crawls beneath the skin. *"Take It All In and Check It All Out"*, *"Lonely Town"* and *"Lonely Street"* are similarly fine tracks with real edge balanced by the joyous celebratory *"When I'm Kissing My Love"* indeed the standard of songs and performance never noticeably drop from start to finish.

90. Rahsaan Roland Kirk

The Case of the 3 Sided Dream in Audio Color (1975)

Rahsaan Roland Kirk was, throughout his career, a very underrated talent. For many his showmanship obscured his musical gifts and he came to be regarded as a huckster selling a gimmick as he would perform on two horns simultaneously. Yet he was deadly serious about his music, and was always willing to use it as a vehicle of expression to make political statements and express his pride in his Afro-American culture. Utilising contemporary Soul music as a base to work from lessened his Jazz purity for the stuffy self-appointed guardians of taste. To them he cheapened the form and was seen as a garish abomination but that view was blinkered and flawed. Kirk was an entertainer more akin to Duke Ellington than Albert Ayler. Deconstruction wasn't his thing, he was blessed with innate musicality and was happy to display his melodic gifts, albeit through a surrealistic prism, while he shared a streak of irreverent madcap humour coupled with self-belief in his music with Charles Mingus, with whom he played in the early Sixties. This fine album displays his free thought process in every aspect from the cover art, through to the choice of material and the fact that on its original release this two-disc set contained three sides of material with the fourth left blank as if to say "I refuse to fit formatting".

The album begins with a robot-voiced higher entity engaged in conversation with Kirk instructing him to dream and the artist declaring he's done with dreaming since a dream aged fourteen about a woman making love to a computer, (most prescient for 1975!). There are two readings of *"Bye Bye Blackbird"* the first light and airy, the second more sombre with deep bass underscoring it. R&B classic *"High Heel Sneakers"* is a New Orleans style funky romp that could almost be The Meters and Scott Joplin's *"The Entertainer"* – it opens with cry baby guitar and is taken as a Blues piece before, at its mid point, Kirk takes it in a different more free direction playing lick after delicious lick and weaving tones together. This track is revisited in a more up-tempo style. Between tracks we hear church bells ringing, cannon shot, ghostly voices and trains thundering past as well as more dream related dialogue that mirrors the restless nights of overactive minds and Kirk's defiant refusal to do as he is commanded. Kirk's self-written pieces are eclectic too, from the James Brown-like *"Freaks for the Festival"* another two version piece with a delightfully eccentric flute solo to the elegant *"Portrait of Those Beautiful Ladies"* which again is reprised and the strut of *"Echoes of Primitive Ohio and Chilli Dogs"* replete with howling canines. Listening to the album in its entirety feels like tripping along wearing Kirk's shoes and being in the privileged position of having access to his vivid imagination. It is a wondrous gift to be treasured.

91. Free

The Free Story (1973)

At the time this career-spanning compilation album was released, the recently disbanded Free were much loved and respected, although that had never been transmitted into huge sales.

Through the decades their reputation has diminished, along with that of other outfits who utilised the Blues as a base from which to operate. Think Peter Green's Fleetwood Mac for instance. While retrospective thought sees the head-banging heavy rock of Black Sabbath, Led Zeppelin, Uriah Heep et al as sonically adventurous and groundbreaking, it does Free a great disservice. They were one of those one-in-a-million aggregations where their unique chemistry added up to a whole, much bigger than the sum of their parts. That's not to suggest that they were weak individually, Simon Kirke was an unshowy rock-solid drummer of great quality, while Andy Fraser, only fifteen when the band was formed, was a fluent inventive bass player, Paul Rogers an underrated guitar player and a supremely gifted singer and Paul Kossoff channelled raw emotion through his guitar playing where he made economy and taste his priority.

To regard Free as a blues band does them no favours, only their first album really utilises that sound, after that the shackles came off and they would add many facets to their sound. To me they were fundamentally a Soul band in Rock band attire. Free grooved, they didn't need gimmicks and had no image. The individuals mentioned above took the same philosophy into the bands they formed after Free; Kossoff's Back Street Crawler, Fraser's Sharks and Bad Company (which contained both Rogers and Kirke) – they never approached Free in terms of quality but such was the integrity of these individuals that the easy option of putting the original band back together was thankfully never entertained.

The Free Story is chronological in concept with each album represented from debut *Tons of Sobs* to the against all odds brilliance of *Heartbreaker* recorded after Fraser's departure and in the midst of the fragile Paul Kossoff's deterioration and dependence on heavy narcotics. *"Mourning Sad Morning"* and *"Heavy Load"* are standouts on side one, both graceful lamentations that display the emotional heart of the band. Side two is devastatingly brilliant, opening with the title track from third album *Fire and Water* before the *Highway* album is represented by the pain of *"Be My Friend"* the strutting bravado of *"The Stealer"*, a live staple for notable Free admirers The Faces, and the deep Soul of *"Soon I Will Be Gone"* before the finale of the swaggering *"Mr Big"* from *Free Live*. The only cover track is Stax Records classic *"The Hunter"* which opens side three and becomes the definitive version, although Ike and Tina Turner ran them close. *"Just For the Box"* from the *Kossoff Kirke Tetsu and Rabbit* album. *"Lady"* by Paul Rogers and *"Peace"*, both recorded in the 1972 band hiatus, only emphasise the strength of the parent unit. Side four delivers up classic singles *"My Brother Jake"* and *"Little Bit of Love"* as well as the thinly-veiled pleas to the ailing Paul Kossoff to address his problems in the soulful *"Sail On"* and the poignant and sad *"Come Together in the Morning"*. Free really were one of the classic bands of the Seventies, they should be remembered fondly.

92. Cecil Taylor
Unit Structures (1966)

Cecil Taylor was a complex and unpredictable individual who made music that reflected his nature, but while intense and challenging, the assertion that it was unfriendly is way off the mark – there is much pleasure to be had listening to the man's music. One has to open the mind because there is nothing that is comfortably familiar to make things easy on the listener. It is uncompromising in its intensity and so far ahead of the curve as to be unique. This recording, made as the Free Jazz movement was in full swing, goes way beyond what the likes of John Coltrane, Albert Ayler or Ornette Coleman were doing with their own highly innovative music where they are taking a giant leap in terms of stretching the parameters of what Jazz could be and exploring the possibilities within that idiom. Taylor's music cannot be contained within those same parameters, he is beyond what is recognisable. His enquiring mind had absorbed the European classical avant-garde experiments of the likes of Karlheinz Stockhausen and mixed it with his love of what Charlie Parker and Dizzy Gillespie had done as they moved the music from the orthodox into the Bebop era. Taylor created a synthesis of these disparate elements to make music no one had heard before, it wasn't designed to be user-friendly and it's certainly not for everyone but it is undoubtedly the work of a musical genius and this album is a head-expanding, dizzying piece of work that is a thrilling listen.

This was the first of a pair of albums released by Blue Note in 1966, the other *Conquistador* is equally magnificent. It was his first since 1962 and there would be no more releases until 1973. It is ferocious and vividly coloured, Taylor plays the piano with intricacy and simultaneous brutality; hammering out flurries of notes in dense clusters while the music is without doubt cerebral. It is performed passionately and is extremely physical, to this end Taylor's unit of Eddie Gale on trumpet, Ken McIntyre on alto sax oboe and clarinet, bassists Alan Silva and Henry Grimes with drummer Andrew Cyrille add power and shades and Jimmy Lyons on alto sax is given free rein to improvise wildly. I can't recommend this album strongly enough to those who enjoy adventure.

93. Mott the Hoople
Mott the Hoople (1969)

Under the tutelage of maverick producer Guy Stevens, Mott the Hoople were created when he took a shine to a band called The Doc Thomas Group but not to their singer, one Stan Tippins. A podgy bespectacled Ian Hunter was chosen as the new frontman and pianist, given a pair of shades and put on a diet. Stan became road manager. While incarcerated at Her Majesty's pleasure for drug offences, the amphetamine crazed Stevens read a novel titled *Mott the Hoople* and decided it was a perfect name for a band he was conceptualising, who would combine a Dylanesque style with a Rock & Roll outlaw swagger.

The band were duly rechristened, much to their initial horror, and before Hunter had even played a gig with his band mates, they were thrust into a recording studio to put together this their debut album and start the journey that would see them build a small but devoted following that unfortunately couldn't sustain them. Then a saviour arrived in the form of David Bowie who gifted them his song *"All the Young Dudes"* which launched them to a couple of years of pop stardom coupled with disagreements and eventually an acrimonious parting.

It was hard not to love Mott, they couldn't be cool if they tried and for all the wrappings of Bacofoil like threads and preposterous high-heeled boots, there was always something provincial about them. Somehow they stayed ordinary, in love with the idea and playing the part of Rock & Roll stars without convincing anybody, least of all themselves. The Rolling Stones they were not, (thank goodness), Mott were touchable flesh and blood, fallible and a fabulous exciting night was guaranteed if you crossed paths with them.

The Kinks *"You Really Got Me"* is scorched through without vocals, it feels like it might crash at any moment. It has edge and is a perfect opening track, two more covers follow; Sir Douglas Quintet's *"At the Crossroads"* and Sonny Bono's, *"Laugh at Me"* both with the Dylan-patented quicksilver sound very evident and Ian Hunter's *"Backsliding Fearlessly"* does not deviate from the template, it's derivative but highly atmospheric and delivered with passion by singer and musicians alike. The first of Mott's anthemic classics gets side two underway; *"Rock and Roll Queen"* penned by Mick Ralphs with a riff The Rolling Stones would borrow for their own *"Bitch"* a couple of years later. Ralphs writes *"Rabbit Foot and Toby Time"* as well which, in truth, sounds like an unfinished idea for a song and really shouldn't have made the cut. Co-written with Hunter *"Half Moon Bay"* restores the quality and if, at over ten minutes, they are overreaching themselves, better that than dumbing down and playing safe – it is a beautiful piece with a haunting quality despite its length. Guy Stevens contributed the final track *"Wrath and Wroll"* an instrumental that doesn't overstay its welcome and sounds like Jerry Lee Lewis jamming with The Velvet Underground which is a nice way to finish this fine, often neglected, album.

94. Kevin Coyne
Marjory Razorblade (1973)

I first encountered Kevin Coyne on the excruciatingly lame BBC2 TV programme *Old Grey Whistle Test*. He must have enlivened proceedings, which usually ranged from the disappointingly dreary to the completely dismal, because even now at a distance of forty-five years I can still picture him; unkempt, dangerous and exciting, his face contorting into that of a leering gargoyle as he spat out words in an unadorned rasp that weren't in the least banal. This marked him out along with the wrenched out noises from a guitar with which he seemed barely acquainted. He was a liberating sight and the first time I realised there was the possibility of making music without a university education or being a self-absorbed virtuoso or having very wealthy parents. The clueless host whispered platitudes and concluded it was "nice", which rather missed the point. I whispered an abusive expletive at the television set, something had changed inside me and Kevin Coyne was the cause. Kevin Coyne was fucking great!

Coyne had been a psychiatric nurse and drug counsellor which informed his thinking and writing. He was deeply compassionate but acerbic; a realist wrestling with injustices, complexities and the emotional fallout of his worldview which in his songs ranged from amusement at the absurdities he encountered, to love coupled with deep despair. Musically his style was Blues derived, but with a surreal edge; he always conjured up for me an image of some nightmarish end of the pier performer, Blind Joe Death in Blackpool perhaps.

This album was his second release by the fledgling Virgin Records following a brutally stripped back solo debut *Case History* and a couple of albums in a band setting as Siren. It is also, despite their being lots of outstanding albums in Coyne's catalogue, his best containing twenty-two tracks across four sides, each one of them quite wonderful, some of the high points being *"Marlene"* a beautiful rolling thing issued as Virgin's first ever single, its B side, *"Everybody Says"*, which is mesmerising and desperately forlorn. The two songs performed on *The Old Grey Whistle Test*, the traditional *"I Want My Crown"* and *"House on the Hill"* a horrifying portrait of the conditions inside a mental hospital. *"Dog Latin"* with a sparse acoustic guitar riff later recycled by The Fall, *"This is Spain"* which is a delicious laceration of tourist attitudes at the time of the package holiday boom, and the splendid romp that is *"Eastbourne Ladies"* another song that picks at a scab to reveal the nasty infection just below the surface. While *"Karate King"* where they go "chop chop in the gymnasium" with Bruce Lee type vocal noises is an absurdist sketch that delights. Kevin Coyne was very special, a great neglected talent, every home should contain one of his albums and given a choice this is the one to choose.

95. Vangelis

See You Later

(1980)

Vangelis initially was a member of early progressive rock band Aphrodite's Child alongside vocalist Demis Roussos. After their groundbreaking album *666* the band split and Vangelis began a solo career creating mostly instrumental albums of sweeping atmospheric grandiosity. He declined the opening left by Rick Wakeman's departure to join English mega star band Yes but forged a working friendship with that band's vocalist Jon Anderson. Film soundtrack work was a logical area for him to move into and he scored big with *Chariots of Fire* and *Bladerunner* and somewhere in the midst of a career defined by a slightly pompous near ambient tastefulness this oddity crept out.

This album was song-based, utilising the voices of Jon Anderson, Cherry Vanilla and Peter Marsh, the experimental music and the concept of a bleak futuristic dystopia are a startling leap into a whole different sphere for Vangelis; never before had he sounded so satirical and hard-edged, never before had he sounded so good either in my opinion although his record label disagreed, pruning two tracks from the record, barely promoting it and neglecting to release it in the USA at all.

Track one, *"I Can't Take It Anymore"* is sung by Marsh through a vocoder, signalling what a radical departure sound-wise this album will be as, over a strung Mike Garson like Avant-Garde piano figure and oriental percussion, the title is repeated over and over cut only by a chorus of "too loud too loud". This is followed by *"Multi-Track Suggestion"* which, while combining a Eurodisco feel with Kraftwerkian elegant synth lines, still manages to convey something ominous and disturbing. *"Memories of Green"* which would be revisited for *Bladerunner* a couple of years later, suggests a sense of alienation and a deep loss carried as it is over a beautiful but mournful piano melody that electronic effects circle and convey menace. The song *"Suffocation"*, inspired by an industrial accident with devastating consequences at a chemical production plant in Seveso, Italy, is chilling asking a series of unanswered questions. The shortest piece *"Not A Bit - All Of It"* has spoken vocals from Cherry Vanilla over a to-and-fro rhythm while the longest track and album closer *"See You Later"* has a chattering machine generated base over which electric piano, guitar and synths swirl, a staccato male choir appear, a child reciting a passage in French and finally Jon Anderson's soaring vocal come and go before the choristers chorus the title with the ever-present question mark evoked once more.

This isn't an easy record to find but I promise it is well worth snapping up if the opportunity arises.

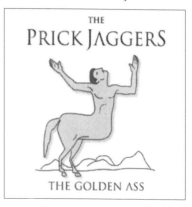

96. The Prick Jaggers

The Golden Ass (2006)

Ask me for my top five favourite Mancunian acts and I might well answer, Roy Harper, 10cc, Buzzcocks, The Fall and of course The Prick Jaggers. People think I'm joking, that I'm being deliberately obtuse, what about Joy Division, Oasis, The Stone Roses, Herman's Hermits, Freddie and The Dreamers, The Smiths? Surely they are better than The Prick Jaggers? Well no, actually they're not.

The collected works of those luminaries don't summon up a fraction of the wit and wisdom displayed on this album by this most unassuming of bands. If you ever saw them perform one of their rare live shows there is every chance you thought they were rubbish and walked out, lots of people did without realising their loss! Rob Jones and Patriq Gannon cut awkward figures when lured onto a stage, more Laurel and Hardy or Gilbert and George than Soft Cell or Suicide. They looked slightly bemused and certainly amused by the prospect of entertaining people, there was absolutely no attempt to adopt some kind of stage presence, no fake emotion, no artifice, they simply stood still and played their songs, audiences mistook this indifference to them as either arrogance or amateurism. I saw Prick Jaggers in Sheffield on what may prove to be their final live appearance. They took the stage to a packed room of around three hundred people, by the end of the first song the numbers had shrunk to thirty as people fought each other to exit the building! Rob and Patriq barely seemed to notice and certainly didn't care one way or another, both of them are smart enough and ego-free enough to realise there are much more important things happening in the world and in our lives than a temporary fix of adoration, they neither require it or desire it, their attitudes inform their music which is a glorious unpretentious intelligent and humorous marvel.

They originally released this album as a lavishly packaged CD that once opened began to rapidly deteriorate leaving fans clinging to a fading memory before the work was rescued by German Shepherd Records who made it available as an indestructible download.

"The Prick Jaggers were once the new Olympian bards of Rock and Roll, they were the voice and promise of the counterculture. They who shat in Hank Marvin's shoe, the guys who put three chords into bed with electronic discharge, who sailed into 2002 and disappeared into a haze of substance abuse, who emerged to find Shergar! They were written off as has beens by the summer of 2005 and suddenly shifted gear releasing their debut album The Golden Ass *in March 2005"*

Thus went the blurb accompanying the album and it was a fair summation of what they were. These days I imagine both Rob and Patriq are slightly embarrassed by this audio ghost of their younger, more callow selves, influenced equally by Dyonsian concepts, Pasolini films and soaking up the atmosphere of a Berlin steeped in history, but also fond of and even a little proud of what they achieved as with minimal guitar and synth, a drum machine with David Wilkinson's Sax adding colour to the wistful *"Virgin Eleousa"* and a mountain of thoughts and words they created a unique masterpiece. All the hits are here, *"Lou Reed's Supper Club"*, *"Love Is a Binary Number"*, *"Alexanderplatz"*, *"Like - Playing a Chinaman In a Racist Pantomime"* and the epic *"I Don't Believe You, (You're a Liar)"* intriguing genius titles to intriguing genius songs.

96. Doll by Doll
Gypsy Blood (1979)

"We are a damaged band from a damaged land" was a sentence once used by Doll by Doll mainman Jackie Leven to describe his band who were one of the absolute finest of all-time and yet meant and continue to mean almost zero to even hardcore music fans.

Formed in London in 1977 from a squatting community riddled with alcoholism, drug addiction and mental health issues, this was a band who would channel their hurt and wounded souls into a music of immense passion and terrifying intensity. They coupled a romantic poetic grandeur with frightening brutality. Leven was not only a genius songwriter but a supreme singer who operated between a velvet croon and operatic highs. The band was taught, tight and tough but flowing as well. They were extraordinary but their approach was far too extreme for the generally genial, happy-clappy pub rock scene. Doll by Doll were angry men who were confrontational and capable of violence and as a result were lumped in with the Punk movement to which they were equally ill-suited; touching thirty they would not have dreamed of lying about their age or dressing up in the latest fashions. The Punks may have feigned a fondness for danger and edge but confronted with hard men with prison time, failed marriages and an appetite for hard drugs behind them, they fled.

The band's debut album, 1977's *Remember* had been excellent, this follow-up totally eclipsed it; it is nothing short of a masterpiece. Riding in on relentless pounding drums, the cautionary tale that is *"Teenage Lightning"* is a full-blooded assault of an opening track, *"Gypsy Blood"* the next track does not take its foot off the throttle, powered by handclaps and featuring near elastic vocals, it is superb.

"Stripshow" is slower but no less gripping with huge swells and crescendos a feature. *"The Human Face"* is a strange psychedelic ballad that breaks into a huge gospel chorus after much ominous lyrical imagery and a guitar break that burns like acid, listening you feel emotionally drained so the beautiful but more restrained *"Hey Sweetheart"* offers some relief with its harmonies and almost flamenco guitar riff before it too roars like a jet engine.

Side two opens with guitarist Jo Shaw's *"Binary Fiction"*, showing he was no song-writing slouch, it is an absolute beast of a track that jolts and jars and the guitar sound achieved is vicious. *"Hell Games"* with the opening couplet of "I lived for a while, in the shadow of castle Frankenstein" has Leven providing an extremely spooked and disturbed vocal. *"Forbidden Worlds"* transports itself from Folk-tinged to darkly psychedelic in an instant, indeed the whole album is a swirling shape-changing epic "I'm sick and tired of the same old song..." sings Leven with an unhinged passion. *"Highland Rain"* and *"Endgame"* share a similar down-at-heel elegance about them but equally both have razor sharp teeth while closer *"When a Man Dies"* finds Leven reciting a brief enigmatic poem by Anna Akhmatova over ripples of guitar ending one of the most hauntingly human albums you are ever likely to encounter.

98. The Beatles

Sgt. Pepper's Lonely Hearts Club E
(1967)

A long time ago my friends
returned from Iceland where
their band, The Fall, had played
some gigs and recorded an
album. The Fall later became the
hippest musical name to drop and they became beyond criticism
but that was not the case back then and they constantly felt they
had points to prove. They were delighted and excited by the music
they'd made for the album which became *Hex Enduction Hour,*
an undoubted classic of their early period. Why I mention this is
because in their bubbling enthusiasm to describe what had been
achieved they referred to it several times as "our *Sgt. Pepper*" which
is instructive. They did not say this is our *Tago Mago, White Light
White Heat* or *Trout Mask Replica,* nor did they did describe it as
being their *White Album, Revolver* or *Abbey Road.* They chose *Sgt.
Pepper* quite deliberately because that album signified a creative
peak, it signified risk-taking, it signified extremely high quality,
that was the esteem the Beatles eighth album generated and it was
held up as the pinnacle of contemporary music making for a long
time before sniping at it became a national sport and the album it
had been hip to love became even hipper to hate.

Instigated by Paul McCartney, who had written the title track
that would feature an Edwardian Brass band, he proposed to his
fellow Beatles they record the album not about *Sgt. Pepper's* band
but as them, this would free them from the expectation of what
a Beatles record should be and open them up to new forms of
creative expression. It was a masterstroke and one replicated by
among others George Clinton in his Dr. Funkenstein alias and
David Bowie adopting the role of Ziggy Stardust. McCartney was

energised, the highly competitive John Lennon was stung into some of his finest work, George Harrison's infatuation with Indian philosophy and musical culture was encouraged and Ringo, the percussive bedrock of the piece, was clearly engaged and never sounded better. The whole package was a revolutionary: the masterpiece album cover by Peter Blake, the printed lyrics, the cut-out moustaches and sergeant stripes as inserts – it raised the standard of what an album could be to unimaginable heights. None of that would have meant much of course if the music had been substandard but contained within was music like nothing that had come before.

Aided and abetted by George Martin The Beatles utilised the studio as a creative tool that had been largely neglected by pretty much everyone. *Sgt. Pepper* was not only a genius record but its audacity and ambition, along with its revolutionary use of sound, changed the face of music inspiring much that was classic; The Kinks, Rolling Stones, The Who, Small Faces, Zombies and The Move in the UK. The Beach Boys, Jefferson Airplane, Crosby, Stills, Nash and Young in the USA and King Tubby and Lee Scratch Perry in Jamaica - all were affected in some way and responded to *Sgt. Pepper.* The four lads who had shaken the world were shaking it again.

It's pointless trying to describe the music, I will presume all are familiar with it, I'll simply reel off these titles: *"Being for the Benefit of Mr Kite!"*, *"She's Leaving Home"*, *"A Day in the Life"*, *"Within You Without You"*, *"Lucy in the Sky with Diamonds"* and *"With a Little Help from My Friends"*... all amazing songs and recordings that it has become fashionable to denigrate, it's laughable really. Consider also that *"Strawberry Fields Forever"* and *"Penny Lane"* were intended for this album before the record company's need for a single saw them used for that purpose.

99. Lord Sutch
And Heavy Friends (1970)

Throughout the Sixties Screaming Lord Sutch, or Dave to his friends, managed to have a kind of career and a kind of success despite having no discernible musical talent.

What he had instead was bags of front, an inexhaustible ambition, a brilliant backing band in The Savages, who at one time or another could count future heavyweights Keith Moon, Nicky Hopkins and Ritchie Blackmore in their ranks. Record-producing fellow traveller Joe Meek provided him with a clutch of heavy-on-the-sound-effects schlock horror singles that, while never coming close to giving him a hit, defined his style as a kind of Music Hall pantomime villain that when unleashed before a live audience was a winner in terms of, as Sutch put it, "putting bums on seats". Screaming Lord Sutch knew the value of publicity, good or bad; he didn't care as long as the press covered it. To that end he formed his Teenage political party to go head to head with PM Harold Wilson at the 1966 general election. He lost, of course, but not at all put out Sutch went on to form The Monster Raving Loony Party and contested and lost deposits in elections all over the UK up until 1997. He was a maverick and an eccentric and difficult not to love a little. Still, by the late Sixties that goodwill was not sustaining a viable career in the U.K. so on a wing and a prayer Sutch headed for Hollywood and drew attention to himself by dressing as a genuine English toff and cruising along Sunset Strip in a Rolls Royce festooned in a giant Union Flag. Miraculously his chutzpah paid dividends and he landed a recording contract with the mighty Atlantic Records home of Aretha Franklin, Crosby, Stills and Nash, and the big new thing: Led Zeppelin. Washed up at home, Screaming Lord Sutch was going to make his first ever album in the USA!

How he did it nobody knows but somehow Jimmy Page and John Bonham were lured into the studio with him. They later claimed it was just for a fun jam and nothing serious as no music was going to be released. That was not how Sutch saw it; he had half of the hottest act in the world playing with him and he was going to exploit the situation to its fullest, in next to no time six tracks were recorded before Page and Bonham scarpered. To make up a full album Sutch decided to use tracks already cut in London, they were much thinner sounding and utilised completely different personnel something that would sound jarring when the record was released. When the album was released Jimmy Page was quick to issue a statement distancing himself from it and reviews savaged it, pointing out with some justification that Sutch couldn't sing and the musicians sounded sloppy and unrehearsed. It didn't chart and in 1989 it topped a BBC poll as the worst album of all time.

To my mind, people often miss the point and my motto of "critics be damned" has served me pretty well over the years. This is a great Rock & Roll record; raw, human, funny, warts and all and honest. If you like The Troggs or The Stooges, you will love this album. The lyrics are simplistic and often plain dumb, Page and Bonham are unrestrained. Sutch shouts tunelessly and out of time, the production is shambolic, it's fantastic! "Flashing lights that shine so bright, flashing lights in the night…" hollers Sutch clearly having a great time, while the Zeppelin crew hammer away at the riff, obviously attempting to get this over and done with quickly. There's not "A Bustle in the Hedgerow" or "A Spring Clean for a May Queen" anywhere in the vicinity and the record is all the better for it. *"Gutty Guitar"* is, if anything, even more simplistic but when Jeff Beck cuts loose on a sonic powered guitar, solo sparks fly. *"Thumping Beat"* literally employs a thumping beat and *"Union Jack Car",* though a quite ludicrous song set to a stolen Chuck Berry riff, is somehow redeemed by the brutality inflicted upon it. *"Would You Believe"* and *"L-O-N-D-O-N"* are properly constructed songs that move you, the former with glorious backing vocals and the latter with a Kinks-like Staccato riff and a chorus as camp as Christmas. Things slow down for the almost Psych *"Brightest Light"* which is almost pretty except it sounds as if it was recorded by the criminally insane. *"Baby Come Back"* finishes the record, it's very silly but has a killer power chorded chorus that always catches me off guard.

Sutch was soon back in the place of his birth where he truly belonged. It was easy to get to see him, his gigs were often in tiny back street pubs of ill repute and he never short-changed an audience as he charged around yelling at the top of his horrible voice while unwittingly causing chaos. There was something of the accidental anarchist about him, he was great fun and they were fantastic nights, that beneath his clown's mask he hid so much sadness that culminated in him taking his own life was truly tragic.

I salute you David! Lord Sutch was a true one off and a character of vivid colours.

100. Root Boy Slim and the Sex Change Band
Zoom (1979)

Root Boy Slim otherwise known as "the Duke of Puke" was born into the higher echelons of monied American Society as Foster Mackenzie III and educated in a series of expensive and exclusive prep schools from which he was expelled before winding up at Yale as a fraternity brother of future President George W Bush before, with relish, they expelled the anti-authoritarian prankster Mackenzie. After graduation Mackenzie drove an ice cream van in Washington where, after a particularly high dose of LSD, he suffered a psychotic break, climbing over the White House gates before being apprehended by security running up the lawn. Explaining to them he was looking for the centre of the universe, he was hauled off to a mental hospital where he was diagnosed as schizophrenic, a condition for which he took medication for the rest of his life.

At this point Mackenzie adopted the name Root Boy Slim and formed the Sex Change Band with a troupe of backing vocalists named The Rootettes, playing in a Memphis Blues Style with Root Boy seemingly permanently drunk or in a drug-induced haze, they built up a strong live following. They were certainly different; Root Boy was fat and greasy-haired and his songs either storyboarded his colourful life or wickedly satirised American society. If you dug Funkadelic or The Mothers of Invention then Root Boy Slim and the Sex Change Band were speaking your language and adding a grooving boogie shuffle into the vocabulary.

Zoom was the band's second album released by Miles Copeland's IRS label and is prime Root Boy. Kicking off with *"World War III"*, which is hammered out gleefully and concerns itself with Jesus cooking barbecue sauce amid a nuclear war. *"Do the Gator"* is a spiritual cousin to The Velvet Underground prototype *"Do the Ostrich"* in its lampooning of dance crazes. *"Loneliest Room in the World"* has Root Boy in confessional mode as in a croon close to Barry White he sings, "I tried marijuana, cocaine and heroin but they couldn't seem to get the thought of you from under my skin". *"Dare to Be Fat"* is a gem and a gauntlet thrown down to image fascists. The most uncomfortably funny and satirical track here though has to be *"Motel of Love"* where a couple unwittingly book into an establishment that caters to exotic sexual tastes. While on *"Sugar Daddy"* he details a sordid tale of a man offering a helping hand which comes with very exploitative conditions. There really is much on offer here to recommend; this is a great album, the Sex Change Band may have been crazies but they were superb musicians and Root Boy sure had plenty to say in interesting ways.

101. Metal Urbain

Les Hommes Mort Sont Dangereux (1980)

I fell in love with Metal Urbain on first hearing. They had seized the possibilities open to them by the coming of Punk and twisted the anger and attack into something uniquely their own. They made something that looked to the future and rather than cling to a limited palette of second hand clichés, they distorted their guitars as they played pummelling riffs. Dispensing of a traditional rhythm section, which in the Seventies was an extremely radical concept, they replaced it with a drum machine and sheets of synthesiser generated noise over which the singer panted and spat out lyrics the contents of which I have to admit are lost on me as a non-French speaker. France boasted next to no Punk scene and as a consequence the outstanding act of their generation were only ever an extremely marginal blot on their home country's musical landscape.

In the UK they were the first act to release music on Rough Trade Records and were championed by BBC DJ John Peel but made no inroads towards even moderate commercial success. Maybe they were too wild sounding and experimental for the sheep-like herd digging the dreadful Drones or the ludicrous Lurkers? But even retrospectively their reputation has never really grown to where it deserves to be. While the later DAF and Chrome are respected as innovators, Metal Urbain remain a relatively undervalued quantity.

The band concentrated on live work and single releases and this album rounded up their first period between 1976 and 1980 when splits in the ranks began to occur. Sleeved, as all their records were, in bold red and black designs with a title that translates as "dead men are dangerous", this fifteen-track record was a collection of their previously released singles and radio sessions. It is stark and brutal, with the hissing synth tones giving it a decidedly futuristic feel, it pounds and pounds unrelentingly like a piston driven sledgehammer and yet it is not unmusical. Melodies weave their way around the rhythms that stick in the ear so you may find yourself humming them as you jerk back and forth remembering the beat that accompanied them. The three singles are of course magnificent and have never aged, they still sound dangerous, edgy and riotous whilst simultaneously jubilant; *"Hysterie Connective"* is track one and *"Panik"* and *"Paris Marquis"* are tracks five and ten respectively but there is no temptation to skip to these better known songs as the quality elsewhere is equally high, if not better. Certainly *"Lady Coca Cola"* and *"Ultraviolence"* are utterly devastating pieces of work that clearly influenced the likes of Big Black in their precise machine-driven assault.

102. Stealers Wheel

Stealers Wheel (1972)

Stealers Wheel are condemned to be remembered, if at all, as some drippy middle-of-the-road outfit who somehow got lucky with the classic *"Stuck in the Middle"*. Alas, my opinion will not alter that misconception but it is so far from the truth and unjustified that it's a puzzle as to how that came to be the accepted truth because one listen to this debut album by the band makes a mockery of that lazy assumption.

What we are presented with is nothing short of a Power-Pop masterpiece that, had it been recorded by a hipper outfit such as Cheap Trick, Big Star or The Raspberries would regularly top best-of lists and be held in stratospherically high regard. Perhaps it's because those bands hail from the USA where it's somehow more acceptable for them to proudly display their Beatles influence whereas home-grown acts like Stealers Wheel and the similarly neglected Badfinger were treated with suspicion and some hostility.

Stealers Wheel were essentially the core duo of Joe Egan and Gerry Rafferty, friends from their teenage years in Paisley and although Rafferty would go on to solo success after the band's acrimonious split, at this stage Egan was the more prolific songwriter and this band had great songs. The album was superbly and tastefully produced by song writing legends Jerry Leiber and Mike Stoller with former Beatles engineer Geoff Emerick. Between them they provide a warm but natural sound for the songs to be best displayed, never taking them into the territory of mushy sentimental gloss. *"Stuck in the Middle"* is of course here but the fact that it is not the stand-out track on the album indicates how high the quality is. The opening and closing tracks are both superlative songs and performances and, as with *"Stuck in the Middle"*, the Egan/Rafferty co-written *"Late Again"* is a stark meditation on a failing relationship and conflicting emotions, while *"You Put Something Better Inside of Me"* is a hymn of thanks and appreciation for the friendship received when life seems harsh. Elsewhere *"Another Meaning"* is a bittersweet Folk concoction with a tropical lilt, that is followed by the albums one misstep in *"I Get By"* a rocking put down of "The Man" dated by its early Seventies usage of "fancy cigar, fast car…" imagery. However Rafferty's *"Outside Looking In"* redeems that track and his vocal positively aches as he ponders some of life's big questions, the brutal fade-to-end track is unwelcome though. *"Johnny's song"* which opens side two approaches Stevie Wonder territory and *"Next To Me"* is sweetly soulful while *José* is a shapeshifting song of encouragement and *"Gets So Lonely"*, a delicate and sad lament played on electric piano, is fragile and deeply human. This is an album of great range and intelligence, it showcases skilled songwriters displaying their craft to superb effect; its neglect borders on the criminal.

103. Subway Sect

Sansend (2002)

Subway Sect were one of the first bands to step into the space opened up by the emergence of The Sex Pistols in 1976, not that they played copycat Punk Rock music rather, like fellow travellers Buzzcocks, The Slits and The Fall, they borrowed punk's tools to invent something entirely different and uniquely their own. It was touched by genius, avoiding cliché (both musical and lyrical) it was idiosyncratic, stripped of any macho posturing, smart and funny (too smart and funny some might say) because as the floodgates opened Subway Sect were swamped by a deluge of soundalike dullards with fake snarls plastered across their pretty boy faces and clenched fists pumping the air in communion with an audience happy to be served up phoney rebellion rather than something new. It must have been disappointing and dispiriting and soon the original group was no more leaving writer and singer Vic Godard with the name that he would use when the music was collaborative as it was on this ignored classic.

Vic had followed his muse as the Eighties had begun, re-styling himself as a crooning torch singer and making some great music that was taken less than seriously, he found himself trivialised and treated as a novelty. What was the point? So he retreated and got on with real life before surprisingly re-emerging with the 1993 Edwin Collins produced *End of the Surrey People,* it was a wonderful album and a mere five years later *Long Term Side Effect* came along, again produced by Collins and was full of easy going charm. Having eased himself back into the habit of recording, this next album took a predictably idiosyncratic turn. Beats and sample heavy, *Sansend* is an absolute delight; it is multi-styled with some of Vic's best writing to date and it sounds like all involved were having a wonderful time bouncing ideas around. It is an album full of high points that defy expectations coloured by imaginative flourishes at some points. We get Vic rapping and clearly relishing the freedom – it sounds like Tony Hancock fronting De La Soul, that is to say it is quite magical. This is a truly collaborative record with three different lead vocalists, between track interjections from Hamish Brown and the beats provided by Nick Brown.

"Back in a Void Again" is Subway Sect par excellence and has Vic's patented laconic drawling over a guitar that adds to this song what Robert Fripp contributed to David Bowie's *"Heroes"*. "Money come in like a trickle and flow out like a flood" Vic observes on *"Nothin is Easy"* and *"Lazy So and So"* paints a picture of a desultory but charming wastrel. *"Go Against the Grain"* and *"The Writers Slumped"* seem to be observations on the bumpy career of the Sect but are wonderfully set, the latter having a Bhangra feel. *"Don't Take It All Out on Me"* is sung soulfully by Chantelle Lamond with an early on record appearance by Holly Cook backing her, while Simon Rivers is given the microphone for *"Turn Your Back on Everyone"* – both are excellent. *"Drop a Bomb on 'Em"* is a wistfully wise commentary on American trigger happy diplomacy. Unspoken love in the face of a coming war is the subject of *"Everything's Crashing Down Around Us"* which has a nagging crash, bang, wallop chorus. *"At the Circus"* is carried along on a beautiful Eastern European-like Folk melody and the final track *"Heavy Heavy Load"* sung by Reggae veteran Larry Marshall, though a little heavy on the vibro slap, has a delicious Lovers Rock groove. Quite possibly the finest album in Mr Godard's undervalued career, *Sansend* is a blast from start to finish.

104. Bread
Bread (1969)

The absolute epitome of safe, bland, adult-oriented, soft rock for people who wore brushed denim and suede in a tasteful combination, *Bread* were guilty of many crimes against music, not least inspiring the ultra-insipid Eagles to douse any residual hot coals in the belly during the corporate Rock machine's heyday of the soporific Seventies. The mere mention of the state of California made me want to vomit, its lauded music scene was smug, phoney, dreary and Bread had been the catalyst for much of what I despised, nonetheless I somehow maintain a soft spot for this album. Their debut was released on the same label as debut albums by The Stooges and the MC5. Now I'm not going to state a case that Bread were as incendiary as either of those acts but the music on this first album is surprisingly sprightly, indeed a couple of tracks here in their chord progressions and chugging beats coupled with picked acoustic guitars echo *Forever Changes* era Love.

The band were made up of David Gates, who wrote half the album, and Robb Roger who, with James Griffin wrote the other half, they were superbly crafted little nuggets influenced by The Byrds and Buffalo Springfield and sweetened by incorporating the melodic approach of Paul McCartney and The Bee Gees - it produced this gem of an album. Beautifully ornate, it fell largely on deaf ears at the time. It is a diverse set of songs, lovingly arranged with imaginative vocal harmonies supporting strong leads featuring soaring falsettos and a bright urgency that would never be replicated. Guitars cascade, the bass is used melodically and piano and organ alternately add rhythmic flourishes and a dash of the groovy to proceedings. However *"Dismal Day"*, the album's lead single, got nowhere in the wake of the band's commercial breakthrough. *"It Don't Matter To Me"* deservedly became a big hit, although it doesn't threaten to overshadow the lesser known songs here on this sunshine-drenched late Sixties pop classic. Time has not lessened the disdain in which Bread are held in but for any fans of Crosby, Stills and Nash and Moby Grape on one hand and Big Star and Badfinger on the other, I'd suggest prejudice should be set aside for you might find much to enjoy here, even though much abuse and scorn may follow... (I speak from experience)!

105. Queen
Sheer Heart Attack (1972)

There are a lot of reasons to dislike Queen. The snobbish "No Synthesisers!" qualification with which they adorned their record sleeves. Their breaking of the cultural embargo on Apartheid era South Africa by taking the coin to play to segregated audiences at Sun City, the ruthlessly cynical usage of *Live Aid* to deflect criticism and re-establish their brand and rid themselves of pariah status. The atrocious Bohemian Rhapsody. Brian May's perm! In naffness terms Queen have only ever been matched by Cliff Richard and The Wombles and yet, like it or not, Queen were a fabulously creative unit who made some quite brilliant records.

Sheer Heart Attack was the band's third album and their breakthrough in both commercial and artistic terms as they left their hard-rocking heavy metal sound behind which was a vile combination of Led Zeppelin bombast and Yes style lyrical pretentiousness, and incorporated a more pleasing pop sensibility into their sound. They had been touring as support act to Mott the Hoople and picking up a few tips along the way when Brian

May was taken ill and hospitalised with hepatitis. As unfortunate as that was, it created a pause in the band's schedule where a more considered approach to writing could be facilitated; it was well used as each member of the band was a more than capable songwriter and the material here was far superior to what preceded it.

Brian May's *"Brighton Rock"*, the album's opener, signals the changes that have taken place, though instrumentally it follows the then recognisable Queen pattern; it is more skittish and playful and the guitar soloing is interesting and experimental rather than dense and predictable. Mercury's *"Killer Queen"* is next and here the formula is completely abandoned in a piano-led romp that became the band's second British but first international hit and was the moment the flamboyance of Mercury began to come to the fore. *"Tenement Funster"*, *"Flick of the Wrist"*, *"Lily of the Valley"* is a three song melody which displays the versatility of the band in moving effortlessly between styles, it is also the first indication of the high regard that the music of 10cc had on Queen and the subsequent debt they would owe to that band. *"Now I'm Here"*, another hit penned by Brian May, reminisces about the Mott the Hoople tour in highly dramatic fashion, *"Stone Cold Crazy"* is Speed Metal before Speed Metal was invented and was subsequently covered by Metallica. John Deacon's *"Misfire"* is melodic and light and *"Bring Back That Leroy Brown"* is Mercury appropriating Ragtime for a good natured romp. *"She Makes Me"* is sung with great tenderness by Mercury over a drum march and strummed acoustic guitar; it is quite lovely and takes us to the final track *"In the Lap of the Gods... Revisited"* which is unconnected to a track with which it shares that title earlier on the record, this is the first attempt at creating a grandiose, melodramatic showstopper in the manner of the later *"We are the Champions"*.

106. Glen Campbell

Reunion: The Songs of Jimmy Webb

(1972)

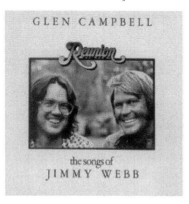

As a pre-teen child there was a type of song that captured my attention and drew me into its narrative, a song that transported me somewhere out of my own limited world and gave me a taste of places and emotions beyond my sphere of reference. The unbearable drama and sadness of Roy Orbison singing *"It's Over"* sent shivers down my spine, Gene Pitney's *"24 Hours from Tulsa"* had a similar effect, whilst Johnny Cash dead-panning through *"Folsom Prison Blues"* was full of forbidding as was Glen Campbell's interpretations of Jimmy Webb's *"Galveston"*, *"By the Time I Get to Phoenix"* and best of all *"Wichita Lineman"* gave me a taste for these seemingly mythical romantic places I could only picture in my mind; they coloured my imagination, they were fantasy lands populated by sad lonely singers with amazing golden voices who looked nothing like the people within my immediate orbit. This album came out when I was seventeen and on the cusp of manhood and though it was not a real reunion as promised by the record's title, it was perhaps even better. Glen Campbell had recorded the definitive versions of a handful of Jimmy Webb songs in the past but they had never actually worked together, now for the first time they were in the studio together, Campbell singing, Webb producing and arranging.

To say I was underwhelmed on first listening to the resultant album is an enormous understatement, nothing pulled me out of my world and into theirs; it sounded, flat, tired and worst of all old. Thankfully I gave it a second chance and then more chances to find that my persistence paid off and the record opened up revealing more and more on each listen. It is understated for sure but there is plenty of depth, it's a subtle suite of songs that reward patience in the listener when their emotional heart is located.

Strangely the album doesn't open with a Jimmy Webb song but Little Feat's Lowell George's *"Roll Me Easy"* presumably because they wanted to start the album in an upbeat manner to which none of the Webb songs were suited. Elsewhere also is Susan Webb's' achingly beautiful *"About The Ocean"* the other eight selections being the work of the advertised writer. The mix of steel guitar and strings is utilised a good deal and with Campbell's rich voice on top of them the record has a widescreen cinematic quality bringing to mind fields of corn beneath the setting sun.

Standouts are the classic *"The Moon's a Harsh Mistress"* and the side two opener *"Ocean in His Eyes"* and *"You Might as Well Smile"* where Campbell sounds at once wise but terribly world weary. He truly was a remarkably intuitive singer, capturing the nuances of each line and delivering totally believable emotional performances without recourse to grandstanding and of course Webb's songs fit him like a glove. This is not an easy record to find, it wasn't a hit and the record label probably viewed it as an artistic indulgence but it is well worth hearing, I guarantee. A year later came *"Rhinestone Cowboy"* brought Glen Campbell superstar status but lost him any semblance of respect into the bargain... Remember him this way!

107. PJ Proby
Heroes (1998)

In my late teens and early twenties I found myself drawn to a book shop just a few doors away from Manchester's Free Trade Hall. It had a peculiar atmosphere that shop. There was something dark and decadent about it; malevolence and corruption was in the air. The proprietors sat stony faced and unwelcoming surveying the comings and goings in their domain, they looked like seedy villains plucked from some esoteric Sixties underground movie. Savoy Books was the name of the shop, it stocked a huge array of Science Fiction, Pop Art and subversive texts as well as a girly mag smut section which drew a flasher-mac crowd and downstairs some records with bootlegs openly displayed. It was a defiantly anti-authoritarian outpost that I loved and where I spent a large chunk of my meagre income both in a thirst for knowledge and in support of these outsiders who, even though I was a regular customer, never offered a hello, thank you or even the hint of a smile.

Through scouring the shelves I discovered Savoy Books was not merely a shop but a publisher and that I liked pretty much everything they published. I first read Brian Aldiss and Michael Moorcock courtesy of Savoy. It was here that I also picked up biographies of Aleister Crowley, Ed Gein and the Marquis de Sade and I also picked up novels by Nik Cohn, which I thought wonderful and through them picked up on the author's fondness for PJ Proby who was held up as the real thing amid a sea of fakes.

I began to pick up his Sixties albums and was mightily impressed and then in the mid Eighties, with Proby himself holed up in a council house in Bury and down on his luck yet still as controversially dissolute and desperate as a man who had once been a huge star breathing the same rarefied air as Elvis Presley and The Beatles could be, Savoy became a record label too with Proby recording a series of singles covering modern day hits including Madonna's *"Into the Groove"* with Madonna herself credited quite untruthfully as backing vocalist. They were cheaply recorded and were never in a million years likely to be hits but they were unafraid to ruffle feathers. They were irreverent and somehow slyly seditious. A decade later they were collected along with other tracks, presumably from the same sessions, and issued as this album.

We get Mickey Newbury's classic *"American Trilogy"* delivered with even more exaggerated emotion than Elvis summoned up. Vegas-era Elvis is evoked again on Bruce Springsteen's *"I'm on Fire"*, then there is a completely bonkers *"Pools of Thought"* that segues into the sacred cow that is Joy Division's *"Love Will Tear Us Apart"* given a drum and bass heavy almost disco treatment with the melody forgotten. Great stuff but better still is the clattering version of Ed Cobb's Northern Soul classic *"Tainted Love"* which opens with Proby yelping and evoking the spirit of Little Richard. *"In the Air Tonight",* the Phil Collins weepy, collides with a drum pattern similar to A Guy Called Gerald's *"Voodoo Ray"* while Proby delivers an almost Gospel vocal performance completely reshaping the horrible original. We move from that deconstruction to Irish Rebel song *"The Old Fenian Gun"* in which Proby sings in an exaggerated Texan drawl to recount the tale over a booming bass noise with not a pipe nor fiddle in earshot removing the dark tale from its original narrow concept and making it universal. *"Sign of the Times"* takes huge liberties with Prince's apocalyptic lyric and barely features Proby. David Bowie's *"Heroes"* has a magnificent vocal that while reshaping the song retains much of the wonder of Bowie's performance, it is a great track and a testament to Proby that he can take material so associated with such an iconic figure and yet interpret it in such a way that he inhabits the song making it less a copy and more an expression of his own personality.

I wouldn't claim this is a faultless album, far from it, but there is a streak of glorious anarchy that runs through it and for that reason I love it

108. The Barmy Army

The English Disease (1989)

To be a football supporter in the Seventies and Eighties was to willingly submit oneself to pariah status. The chattering classes were more than disinterested, they were outright disdainful and the terraces of the dilapidated stadia where the tribal rites of the Working Classes were played out seethed with a passion considered uncouth to the majority of the country. On the field, the Working Class ballet was often sabotaged by the win at all costs mentality of carthorse-like hatchet men. All this was played out under the watchful eye of the police, who one soon realised were manned by brutal psychopathic oafs intent on inflicting violence on the people they were supposedly protecting. It was another perk of the copper's job, along with the overtime, and any regular supporter who avoided being snatched, beaten and hauled before a court on completely bogus charges could consider themselves extremely lucky.

But we loved it, it was a release, an escape from the humdrum, the clubs seemed attached to the communities that followed them and the players were not untouchable pampered superstars but real flesh and blood human beings not totally removed from reality. You envied them rather than resented them. This album captures the last gasp of that era coming in the wake of the disasters at Heysel, Hillsborough and Bradford, in the wake of the Conservative government proposing compulsory identity cards for all football supporters and before Italia '90 where the national team's relative success, "that nice Gary Lineker" and the soap opera that was Gazza captured national attention. This was before *The Taylor Report* instituted the dawn of all seater stadiums and before the creation of the cash hungry Premier League.

Put together by On-U-Sound dub maestro and West Ham fan

Adrian Sherwood, he utilities the formidable talents of Tackhead guitarist and bassist Doug Wimbish and Skip McDonald along with contributions from the likes of Keith Levine and Al Jourgensen to create a funky electronic Hip-Hop sound over which are layered crowd noises and chants, snatches of commentary and post-match interviews; it is at once a homage to the game and a political statement as well as being a marvellous listen no matter what team holds your allegiance. There are tracks about Alan Devonshire, Billy Bonds and Leroy Rosenior of West Ham, Celtic and Scotland's Kenny Dalglish and Brian Clough detailing his "...Clout" administered to an encroaching spectator. *"Civil Liberty"* looks at the identity card debate and *"Mind the Gap"* at the disparity between the haves and have-nots. The snatches of commentary used are particularly delightful coming from an era when there was not much so-called 'expert analysis' but an era when the great commentators truly conveyed the passion, emotion and love of the game we all felt.

109. Family

Fearless (1971)

Every critic thinks he's cool

Man and word precious jewels

Me I've got my own little rules

Belligerent and defiant, Roger Chapman spat these words out on this album. He knew Family were not and never would be press darlings, he knew Family would never have private jets and country mansions, he knew Family would never be viewed as being cool but here they were again all guns blazing with a killer record that would make people listen and confer respect on his beloved band, except of course they didn't listen, didn't want to hear it. There were hipper sounds around; who cared about these oiks from Leicester, possibly the uncoolest town in the UK.

For some reason lots of bands I liked in the early seventies had names that began with the letter 'F'; Fairport Convention, Faust, Focus, Free, Fleetwood Mac, The Faces and Family - of all of those Family were the underdogs who received none of the respect conferred on the others. I adored them even though none of my friends held them in anything like the same esteem. They didn't like Roger Chapman's voice, they said "they look crap they don't rock hard", "they don't do this they don't do that" but I didn't care what my friends thought. I didn't care what they weren't. It was what they were that excited me. For one thing they seemed like ordinary people, albeit creating extraordinary music and, unlike the big untouchable rock stars of the day, you could recognise the members of Family as types you might see having a drink in a pub among the proletariat. If you compared the appearance of singer Roger Chapman; thinning hair, geography teacher beard, rugby shirt and Dr Martens, to that of Robert Plant, Roger Daltrey or Ozzie Osborne in their flimsy chest-baring chiffon blouses, tight crotch-enhancing trousers and snakeskin hipster boots, it was instantly apparent they were worlds apart. Family had a cocky street swagger that seemed genuine and they looked like they could handle themselves if there was any trouble, they were not poseurs and I identified with them immediately.

Fearless was their fifth album and truth be told after the classic debut *Music in a Dolls House* they were drifting for a couple of years. Their albums were good but not great, *Fearless* changed that. Violin-toting bassist John Wieder departed to be replaced by John Wetton from Mogul Thrash after declining an invitation from Robert Fripp to join King Crimson (12 months later he would reverse that decision and leave Family for Crimson). His arrival brought a vibrancy and vitality along with his propulsive playing that revitalised the band and altered the sound considerably. Poli Palmer, the percussionist, shines as he imaginatively enhances the faultless drumming of Rob Townshend. Charlie Whitney is a wonderfully melodic and versatile guitar player and Chapman reins in any grandstanding on the vocal front to let the songs and music do the work.

The sounds incorporate Folk, Blues, barrelhouse piano, muted horns and vibraphone as the moods change between introspection to celebratory to outright deranged on the apocalyptic *"Burning Bridges"* the closing track and a highlight of the band's career. Opener *"Between Blue and Me"* is tender *"Sat'd'y Barfly"* is rollicking while *"Larf and Sing"* is strange indeed. All the songs are strong and the textures rich and intoxicating displaying a flair for drama. Like all great bands Family sounded like nobody else, they were underrated then and their reputation has never posthumously been elevated in the way much lesser peers have benefited from reassessment.

As for me I remain completely smitten.

110. Rod Stewart
A night on the town (1976)

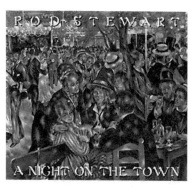

It's one thing to like Rod as part of the Faces and his simultaneous solo career but it's another kettle of fish to find anything nice to say about his American recorded albums that began with 1975's *Atlantic Crossing* or this album released a year later but the truth is his solo career had followed a formula and to one degree or another he had made the same album five times. His first two albums had built towards the absolute triumph that was *Every Picture Tells a Story* before declining slightly on follow-up *Never a Dull Moment* and then dramatically on 1974's *Smiler*.

Something had to change and the decision to relocate to the States was made in the wake of calling time on the Faces who in truth had died the moment Ronnie Lane quit following Rod's unnecessarily negative quotes about the *Ooh La La* album to which

Ronnie had contributed much of the strongest material. There was also of course the fact that a clearly besotted Rod was trailing around after actress Britt Ekland; they made for a nauseous power couple showcased in a period TV documentary that showed them spending obscene amounts on chintzy antique lamps. The couple dressed and made up almost identically; both emerged as charmless and despicable individuals and the fall out was that the opinion of them everywhere between Land's End and John O'Groats was that they were 'a pair of twats'.

The plan was hatched to record an album that would emphasise Rod's love of American soul music. It was produced by Tom Dowd who had an impeccable pedigree having worked with the greats at Stax records, while Stax house band the MGs were to provide musical backing and to embellish the sound a host of other players were added. *Atlantic Crossing* proved to be a huge success, reversing the downward spiral of his albums. It was split into two halves; side one ' fast', side two ' slow' and grudgingly one had to admit it was good if lacking in a bit of heart.

When sessions for *A Night on the Town* began it was with much the same crew of musicians and Tom Dowd retained the producer's chair. This time there was a 'slow' side followed by a 'fast' side, it looked for all the world like, and is often allocated the role of *Atlantic Crossing* Part Two but that's not quite true; for all the similarities there was a crucial difference which was the reintroduction of the folk stylings that had been the platform for Rod's earlier work and was a style where he sounded at his most convincing. The album begins with *"Tonight's the Night"* which was a huge hit single that courted controversy by recounting the taking of a maiden's virginity, it had to be said though that it was not crude or gratuitous rather it was tender and very good indeed. Next up, Cat Stevens *"First Cut is the Deepest"* proved that Rod was a brilliant interpretive singer and he was back with the definitive version of a wonderful song. *"The Killing of Georgie Parts 1 and 2"* was a revelation for many and quite a bold statement for a mainstream artist to make. Cast musically between Dylan in his story-telling folk period and Lou Reed's *"Walk on the Wild Side"* with a hint of disco in the mix, it tells the tale of a Faces fan known to Rod. A gay man is shunned by his family but finds acceptance in NYC before being brutally murdered; it was a tender and sympathetic tribute as well as being in the context of the times thought-provoking in the extreme. *"Trade Winds"* also deserves high praise as it is a moving socially-aware and soulful piece. The fast side isn't as good but still serves its purpose, only one Stewart original makes the cut *"The Balltrap"* which is a lewd sub-Rolling Stones rocker. It is accompanied by two country standards *"Wild Side of Life"* and *"Big Bayou"* which is lifted from the Faces set list, while Manfred Mann's sixties hit *"Pretty Flamingo"* is also performed with celebratory swagger.

A Night on the Town is extremely enjoyable, one didn't have to jump too far into the future for the bum-wiggling spandex-trousered pantomime to begin, much to the horror of innocent bystanders, but that's not a reason to disregard this exceptional album.